Calin Wheeler was a typical kind of guy, who underwent a full spiritual awakening high up the Moroccan Atlas Mountains. The period that followed afterwards would not only leave him a changed man but his understanding of how life worked would help him evolve into becoming a better person.

To all those who have gone before me, and after me, may the light of the Divine shine forever bright, and that your journey home is as rewarding as you would like it to be. Love, peace and joy.

To my parent, to let you know that you did too good a job. To my two brothers, I am and will be the luckiest brother alive.

Calin Wheeler

The Enlightened Self

A Memoir Of Spiritual
Transformation

AUSTIN MACAULEY PUBLISHERS™
LONDON • CAMBRIDGE • NEW YORK • SHARJAH

A CIP catalogue record for this title is available from the British Library.

ISBN 9781035850570 (Paperback)
ISBN 9781035850587 (ePub e-book)

www.austinmacauley.com

First Published 2024
Austin Macauley Publishers Ltd®
1 Canada Square
Canary Wharf
London
E14 5AA

Table of Contents

Prologue

You could say that true spiritual awakening is an inside job that requires assistance from the divine.

I would never call myself a spiritual person by nature—even though I am. Nor did I intentionally and consciously seek a spiritual path by which to live my life.

I came to realise that the spiritual journey I have been on for the past 39 years of my life wasn't planned at a conscious level but more in the realms of the divine.

It was only when I became *fully spiritually awake* did I realise that the thoughts and then the words, combined with the actions that followed, were in turn part of a larger plan that was held within myself, long before I had time to realise the full implications of this.

I am now under the impression, with the awareness that I now have, that I believe all human beings travel this spiritual path, even if they are not consciously aware of it nor fully understand the implications of the journey itself.

I once naively considered that I was living my life on my own terms; meaning a life that was based on my decisions, actions and thoughts, but more importantly, with complete freedom of choice.

I mean, isn't that one of the fundamental principles of being an individual—being able to choose freely and openly for oneself; being able to live life on one's own terms?

What I wasn't aware of was that within each of my decisions was contained what I would like to call small elements of spiritual essence; which, when assessed in an objective way, impacted on the way that I was living my life—physically, mentally and spiritually—without being aware of it until I had "woken up".

Looking back at this now, and having gained a more rounded perspective, I have come to realise that I hadn't really thought about the full ramifications of my choices and the decisions I had made.

If I had known then what I know now, looking back, I wouldn't have made those decisions in the first place, but wouldn't we all at some level say the same?

I can honestly say that when I was completely immersed in living my life as myself, it was incredibly difficult to see the bigger picture. Hindsight is such a wonderful thing, as I came to realise that living in the moment isn't the same as being in the moment.

From pure beingness, all things flow naturally; while living in the moment could be considered just a temporary state of the mind, or a temporary state of being.

During this long spiritual journey that I have been on, I have experienced moments of self-contemplation, insight and self-awareness. It was also during those moments that my mind would stop thinking and I would start to become my more natural enlightened self.

How I was able to achieve this was, and still is, as natural as breathing. Literally, it is as though within each one of us there is this natural ability, God given, to be able to move beyond one's mind.

Since I know that we do this without much effort, the real question is whether a person can do this consciously; and if so, what would a person need to do and be to experience their natural state of being more of the time?

I have found that one of the best ways to quieten one's mind is to be honest with oneself. There is a groundedness when you come from a place of pure honesty and humility. It's as though the wheel of the unseen universe naturally quietens the mind and presents you with choices that you wouldn't have thought of.

You know you have got it right when you can hear life outside you so clearly and the colours are so vivid and bright that there seems to be a sense of liveliness. You have naturally elevated your sense of being, which creates a peace and calmness within you.

It was from these natural states of being that I remembered that I would be able to connect to my soul and review and assess where I was on my life journey in that single moment.

It was like having checkpoints, so that when I arrived at a specific place, a moment or an event, I would then naturally oscillate to that enlightened state of being, so that I could make key decisions to ensure I was on the right path in my life journey.

What I found out later, when I had "woken up", was that what I had been doing was stepping outside physical time, which means moving out of my body, then connecting with the spiritual dimension of life itself, where my soul predominately resides, and then bringing forth those situations in which I would like to have an experience.

Then, in agreement with others spiritual beings, I would elicit them, and vice versa, into this creative process, whereby each one of us would play a role just for that moment in time before moving on to something else.

When connected to my spiritual side or that part of myself that I would call the soul, I would hear a quiet voice within me asking questions like:

Is this something you would like to experience?
And
Are you sure this is the right decision?

Then there would be a brief conversation and an assessment carried out between each one of these key crucial decision points on my life journey, before I moved out of this space and back to reconnect to the mind.

I know now that all human beings create this experience for themselves, and that we are all one in this experience. We are a group of individual souls, who make up a larger collective.

We are also interconnected and at the same time, separated on purpose and by design, so that as individual spiritual beings, we can not only operate separately on different levels, depending on what experience we have chosen for ourselves, but by the same token, we have all enlisted ourselves and each other, so that we can have our own unique tailored experience.

It is divine genius.

This was part of the insight that I gained from my awakening. I had no idea that this was going on; it was intentional. It would take a level of infinite intelligence that is way beyond the understanding of a human mind to figure this out.

You would need to connect to your soul first, since that part of you is also connected as one to the whole of life itself. This is what some have called the connection to the whole of life, by the word or label known as God, or also known by other names.

I also had moments of anger, denial, resentment, fear, hatred, rage and self-loathing.

I can't help but notice, as I review and assess each word, that they contain a level of emotional energy that would move through me, and with this movement, there would be times when I would act as though they were true, and in return, experience the fullness of the consequences that followed.

Some words would lift me up on an emotional high; then, as quickly as I would rise, I would come crashing down.

I also experienced the opposite; there was the feeling of being in love with life, moments of joy and hope, ambition at work. And then there was empathy, and warmth for others. There were also moments of compassion and understanding.

I was able to move outside my own life of dramas and connect to other people. I always found this experience to be grounding; grounding in life, in spirit and in soul.

Anger can also be healthy, when used wisely. I found that the key is not to allow anger to become too overwhelming or a natural default state of mind, especially when you're not being totally honest with yourself.

I also realised that the emotions were an indicator that I was alive and that I cared. Anger is usually a signpost that something is wrong from your own personal point of view; and it is just that, it's only your point of view.

When I have this experience, this feeling of anger, I try to move out of my thinking, so that I can gain a level of objectivity. I have found that when I drop my line of thinking, by changing my focus and attending to where I'm putting my energy, I can easily come back to the present moment. I notice that my anger dissipates instantly through me letting go.

There is nothing great about lying to yourself and to others by trying to live up to an image of something that you're not in the first place.

Overall, this has been an incredible experience, from the moment I heard the divine voice high up in the mountains of Imlil, to the day that I became enlightened as to who and what I am.

It took me years of slowly and methodologically putting together the stages of the process that I went through before I became what I am today.

I came to realise that when you use words and imagery that best describe any experience that you have been through, you can only fit in so much detail as the experience itself is more enriching than words can convey.

Yet, I still struggled to outline what I had experienced, felt and seen. The reason for this is simple. I found the experience to be so profound, so incredible and beautiful for what it was that it became incredibly challenging to describe, especially when it is you going through the experience and not someone else.

Last Call

Dusseldorf, Germany
20 December 2016

I just sat there, staring out of the window from the comfort of my small, but cosy, hotel room, watching the slow drift of rain on a cold miserable December afternoon in Dusseldorf, Germany.

The shining screen of my laptop was temporarily forgotten; the fatigue and vestiges of anger and annoyance were slowly draining from my face, and the tightness of my body slowly loosening as the anger drifted away.

I had just for a moment, however temporarily it may have been, lost my temper with my colleague and friend who also happened to be my boss. I had surprised myself with the raw outburst of emotion, which came out of nowhere.

I hadn't realised till then that the slow and continuous build-up of pressures and stress were incremental in their creation; it had all started early in the year, but had now reached a crescendo and I just had to let it out.

To my relief, I quickly apologised for losing it, since my boss and colleague was also one of my biggest supporters on the project, and she didn't deserve to be on the receiving end of my anger.

I had simply been annoyed and pissed off when she asked for a quick turn-around for a document to be written in less than 24 hours, which would normally require a couple of days to produce any semblance of a professional output.

What she had asked for was part of a long list of unrealistic demands, and today, I had let her know how I felt.

But, deep down inside, as I stared out on that cold winter day, I realised that not only was I acting out of character, since I already knew the request wasn't achievable; but that what really bothered me was that something deep inside me had been stirring for a while.

That stirring was, I knew, already somewhere along the line. I was truly lost; not in my work, but in life in general. The guy that I used to be a couple of years back wouldn't have been in this situation in the first place; I would have had something ready to go.

In fact, not only would I have managed the process better, but also, I wouldn't have received the request since she would already have in her inbox a professionally crafted document with quality information.

I already knew in advance that the project I was working on was a dog to start with; you need to manage that process, and I hadn't done so.

I couldn't shake off the feeling that had been going on in the background for a while, where it had stewed and stirred, endlessly going backwards and forth, like a siren call; and however much I tried, all the king's horses and all the king's men couldn't put Humpty Dumpty together again.

I really didn't know what I had done wrong; or where I had gone wrong.

My anger was a shield of my own making to the outside world; I wanted to be left alone. Now, any image of harmony I had projected at work had been blown away by something within me. I been denying something for so long that I really didn't know what to do, and it scared me.

I knew, even though no one else did, that somewhere, somehow, I had made a mistake many years ago, but for the love of me, I didn't know what it was.

It gnawed at me, slowly and intentionally stripping away my confidence, and in the process, my personal and professional level of competence. I couldn't stop it. I didn't know how.

I had tried so many things, had gone back to so many environments where I had prospered, and met old teachers. The only thing I could latch on to was that somewhere along the line, I had settled for less in life. This bothered me.

Financially, I was in great shape; but emotionally, I was a mess. Physically, I had recovered from ligament damage to my knee and was slowly on the mend. Relationship-wise, I had no energy, no drive or ambition to meet women.

This was a reverse in circumstances from where I had been three years prior. Then, I had been in peak shape, at the top of my game, with an abundance of life flowing non-stop through me. But now it had gone tits up and I was a fucking mess.

Hero to zero, but with no bounce to get back to the top again.

I packed up for the day, realising it was probably in my own best interest. And on top of that, it was Christmas season. Wherever I looked, I was greeted by Xmas trees, flashing lights and dancing Santas, but I wasn't in the mood for any festivity cheer.

I was out of the room, down the lift and headed straight into the lounge bar of the hotel. *Fuck it,* I thought, *I'm now on my Xmas break.*

I'd been so close to finishing off the year without a hiccup. I downed one beer and sat there, patiently waiting for the clock on the wall to tick away.

Next thing you know, I'm out of the hotel bar and heading for the airport. As the taxi made its way, I looked down and read the text from my boss, thanking me and my colleagues for all the hard work we had done this year and to enjoy our Xmas. If I had felt bad before about my outburst, now I felt worse.

Xmas and No Party Cheer

I always enjoyed watching the Xmas and New Year films, *Scrooge* being one of the best, so I was pleasantly surprised that I really enjoyed it. I still remember that I had mastered the art of attentive listening, or my version of it, as I sat there and listened to my parents that Xmas day.

I was surrounded by nephews and my niece. I should be happy, but I wasn't. And I noticed, as I counted down the days before I left to go to warm and sunny Morocco that I just needed to hang in there.

There wasn't anything wrong with the family, they were great; it was me. I knew I needed a break. I needed to reset and recharge. I needed the tad bit arrogant guy to come back, the one who used to have confidence in himself, to laugh at life and myself. All was forgiven.

Scrooge, maybe I was; Bill Murray, maybe. I had put money first. I mean, isn't that what professionals do? You make as much as you can, when you can, regardless of the personal cost.

It always annoyed me and delighted me that while Hollywood seemed to think that it required a woman to save the day, and in his case, his life.

I knew it was corny, cheesy, but it worked; and it's a family film, but that's not how it works in the real world of life. The only person who can save you is you, or so I thought and assumed. Sometimes, my assumptions became my reality.

I slowly made my excuses to the rest of the clan and made my way to my room. Three days to go, I remember thinking. I was there in form, but not in spirit. Sleep came easily that day, and I was pleasantly surprised how quickly those days went.

Soon, I found myself making my way home. London was calling; still in my opinion one of the greatest cities in the world, and site of my humble abode since 2005.

As I entered my flat, I could feel the coldness and emptiness of my surroundings pervade me. It was the opposite of where I had been, where I had been greeted by warmth, love and openness.

But just for a second, I nearly got it; what I got I didn't know, but just for an inkling, there was a flash of recognition, a remembrance of something, but then it was gone. I dropped my bags down, knowing that tomorrow, I was travelling to newer and grander pastures.

I tried my best to recall what I was thinking; it was like a eureka moment, but all I could recall was haze, a sense of something, like a trail of vapour that had disappeared into thin air. *Whatever*, I muttered to myself. Maybe I will remember later, as it couldn't have been important anyway.

The heating kicked in as I packed for tomorrow. It brought a smile to my face to think what I was going to wear, and what would I be donating.

The small glimmer of hope of change, real change as I would later realise, was gone as I went back into my small-minded world.

Part One: Morocco

The start of the adventure

I spent months planning and preparing with my point of contact in Morocco, a senior and easy-going mountain guide called Mo. I had met him on a previous expedition, a couple of years earlier, and we had made arrangements for me to visit the Atlas Mountains that winter.

There I was, moving and weaving through Marrakech airport's arrival area, until I found myself excitedly shaking hands with him. We both smiled. It felt good to be back.

The warm Moroccan air greeted me as we left the airport; a welcome contrast to the bitterly cold wet winter day in London that I had left behind.

I dropped my gear into the boot of the car, and we set off for our destination high up in the Atlas Mountains. My first port of call would be a village called Imlil, where I would stay one night before making my way up to the French Alpine Refuge, which would be my base camp for three nights.

As we drove through the busy streets of Marrakech, I sat back in the car and relaxed, watching the locals thronging about their business.

On my previous visits, I had always found the city to be an amazing and exotic place, with such incredible and charming places to visit and see—especially the world-renowned marketplace, which could quite easily be used as a scene for one of the *Indiana Jones* films.

On this occasion, I had decided not to spend an evening exploring the city, but go directly to the village of Imlil instead and stay the night before making the ascent up the mountains.

Mo informed me that he had some bad news; he had recently broken his foot, so his brother-in-law, also called Mo, would be taking his place and had agreed to the set itinerary. I smiled and said that wasn't a problem, even though I felt disappointed.

I had been looking forward to the banter with Mo from my previous trip. But, since I was in such a good mood, I wasn't going to allow minor things such as a change in personnel to bother me.

As we hurtled out of Marrakech and started climbing towards the Atlas Mountains, I began to think about the difference of going there alone.

This was my third visit to Morocco, and on the previous occasions, I had always been a part of a small tour group of trekkers, whose levels of experience ranged from the amateur to the enthusiast and even to accomplished seasoned professionals who had scaled as high as Everest.

On my first trip, I did the traditional five-day summer Atlas excursion, and I loved it. I had caught the trekking bug ever since then. On my second visit, I was a lot fitter and more focused, and I had found the experience to be so much better.

On this occasion, I had decided to come from a simple need for change and an escape from the norm. I had only recently recovered from knee ligament damage, but I had decided that it was worth the risk and the effort.

The village of Imlil

As we came closer to the mountain range, the sights and sounds of mountain life greeted me. It was wonderful. I could feel my spirits lift with a sense of elation.

As I gazed at the spaciousness between the ridges and contours of the mountainsides, I loved the way they naturally and beautifully flowed into one. I knew that I had made a great decision in going.

We parked up and strolled through Imlil town to Mo's house, where we would spend that evening and the last day of our return.

The food on offer that night had been patiently cooked by Mo's wife and mother and was first class; an array of Moroccan dishes stretched from one side of the dinner table to the other, seeming endless at first.

I gazed across with hunger and eager anticipation at the perfect feast; it was exactly what I needed for the long haul ahead.

I had never eaten as well, and by the end of the evening, I couldn't move. It was wonderful. I now had enough energy coursing through me to run a marathon. We all sampled the home-made Moroccan mint tea, which combined with the rich mountain air to be not only refreshing but invigorating. It went down well, cup by cup.

When I went to my room later that evening, the only thing on my mind was what would be the best combination of clothing to wear for the next day, and what should I leave behind. As the saying goes, 'There's no such thing as bad weather, only bad clothing'.

I also needed a good night's sleep, as the demands of high altitude would play havoc with my energy. This might be my last night of 8 hours' full sleep before returning.

One of the things that I had picked up when travelling on treks across Africa was that mountain gear was at a premium, so I had packed a small bag with all my extra duplicated items separately and would look to donate them later.

Revelation

As I was readying myself to sleep, I could feel the warmth and snugness of my sleeping bag wrapped around my tired body. Then just as I was about to drop off, I suddenly heard a distinct voice right in front of me. It was so clear and loud that it was as though there was someone else standing in the room right in front of me.

I instantly recognised it, this voice that called out to me in the darkness. I had been listening to this voice from the first day that I can consciously remember.

It was the same voice that had spoken to me in the coffee shop a couple of months earlier and had calmed my concerns when I was having a troubling conversation with my friend.

It was the same voice that had also spoken to me when I was being picked up at the airport in Morocco and advised me to go along with the change in plans, even though I had no idea what these changes were or what they entailed.

I knew that voice, as I had known it from the earliest day that I can remember, when I was a child and first heard it.

The voice said, *Hello.*

I replied with, *I know who you are.*

Then, in a single moment, it was as though time itself stopped. I could see a bright white light appear right above my head. I just stared straight at the light, transfixed in awe and trying my best to figure out what was going on.

Then I had this strange thought, at that precise moment. I remember thinking to myself that it felt as if the light had always been there, just hanging right up above me.

That took me by surprise, as it was so obvious to see it and now to be aware of it, but before I could even think again, the light and I became one. In this oneness, I felt a surge of energy, like a stream of information flowing right into me, like a download, and I was able to instantly remember memories that stretched as far back as my early childhood to the current day, all done in an instant.

I felt incredible, and due to the miraculous nature of what had just happened, I also felt completely overloaded. Just a second before the "download", I couldn't wait to go to sleep, but now I found myself rippling with pure energy that radiated throughout my entire being.

I was alive and I felt euphoric. My fatigue had disappeared. I knew that I had connected to something so vast and so powerful, that wasn't me.

Then the light disappeared, and with it, the connection was gone; but what remained in the room was a peaceful and loving presence. I could feel it radiating inside and outside myself at the same time.

I tried to assimilate what had just happened. The closest I can describe is that around the information or data, there seemed to be a layer of spiritual information that resided within each specific moment from my past that I hadn't been previously consciously aware of but now I was. It was life-changing. It was profound.

It also had realism. Not only had a veil been lifted from myself, but I was also seeing with great clarity the reasons why I had been through specific moments in my past in the first place.

Any nagging doubt, or suspicion, or the endless questions "why?" that followed my way of thinking over the course of my life had now been answered. I also knew intuitively why I had made specific choices throughout my life. The revelation was incredible.

As I sat there in my sleeping bag, I found myself instantaneously re-watching and remembering these specific memory moments from my past, re-enacted visually. It was like watching a film of my life in a movie theatre.

I was then shown a small brown book. When I initially opened it, it had only one page of the story, written by my own hand. But then with the download, the rest of the pages of the entire book were now complete.

The left-hand pages of the book held the memories of what I thought had taken place; then the right-hand pages contained all the spiritual elements of what was going on inside me, at a deeper level, which until now I hadn't been consciously aware of.

Now that I became aware of this spiritual detail, it enabled me to view my experience with a level of objectivity that I wouldn't have been capable of. The reason, I noted to myself, was that I was no longer immersed or contained in my own internal world of my past.

I could now see with insight, wisdom and enlightened knowledge all that was pertinent to me through the experiences I had had. I could view the download since I was effectively outside my mind.

With this new spiritual truth, I now knew that my experiences were all relative to myself and to me alone. Also, I could feel a sense of calmness as there was no emotional baggage I might have felt about my memories. It was as though they had been completely removed.

As I watched one of my past experiences, I noticed that it wasn't only happening to me, but through me, and that I had been a willing participant as had others during my life journey. I in theirs, and they in mine.

It was as though the people I had met over the course of my entire life were at some level interconnected with each other.

Not only were we separate from each other, but we seemed to cross over into each other's pathways, so that each one of us could interpret an event at a specific moment in time, so that each had their own individual experience; but we were all in it together as one, though each to their own individual selves was true. As Shakespeare said, "To thine own self be true".

I then realised that I had been using my mind to navigate through these experiences, so that I could experience myself as an individual who was also a part of something bigger. What surprised me was that my mind wasn't aware of this.

It was as though even though you were connected to your mind, yet you were also made up of other parts of yourself, and you experienced the fullness of life based on those parts of yourself that were in the actual experience itself.

Not all my experiences had been enjoyable, and at times this was by design. How else could I have experienced and be able to distinguish the sweet from the sour?

I also knew that I was connected at an individual level to a source that had always been there. This source flowed through every facet and every level of life itself, call it what you want; God, life, energy, the universe, etc.

There are so many names to describe it. I just didn't know it had existed before. Maybe conceptually I could get it, but now I could understand—or better yet, start to understand it.

As I continued to view those moments from my past, I found at times I would catch myself thinking and saying to myself privately, 'The next time I come around, I want to experience more of this and more of that.'

I also remembered that when I caught myself doing this, I would tell myself off and wonder guiltily what I meant and why I would say this in the first place and the meaning behind it. It used to freak me out. So, I would deny it. I would lie to myself.

Now that I knew what was going on, I would literally catch myself being disconnected from my mind; and during those moments, I would reconnect to this source.

Once I was certain about a specific choice or decision that I was about to make, I would then move or oscillate back and reconnect to my mind. I would notice that I was doing it, but I didn't know the reasons behind it, that had been removed.

So I would freak out, thinking that there was something wrong with me when there never was; but because of the feeling, I would want to forget these "little moments" scattered throughout my life journey.

It was deliberate and intentional. Still, the residue, the unique signature, and a faint memory of what had transpired remained in my subconscious.

It was as if I had exited the *Wizard of Oz* machine and then went back to living life as me, without realising what I had just done and the reasons why I had done it in the first place.

Mini Satori

As I sat there at the side of the bed, still wrapped warmly in my sleeping bag, with the download of memories still coursing through me, I started to remember the infamous meditation session that took place eight years ago.

A memory that had remained hidden not so much in my subconscious, but more in a spiritual realm; and now I was being reminded of it through the download.

It had been my first true awakening moment, a mini *satori*. I just sat there in the room and started to remember the experience.

I was 30 at the time, and my flatmate, who was a practising Buddhist, had invited a friend and me to attend a meditation session with her at the local drop-in centre.

I had declined the invitation quite a few times, as it held minimal appeal to me, but then one day, I decided to take her up on her offer as I told myself that I wanted to have a new experience.

I vividly remember coming across an article in a magazine about how be open to new experiences, so I decided to go for it; I mean, what was the worst that could happen?

When I arrived at the temple, I found myself experiencing a quiet and relaxed atmosphere and I instantly liked it. It was a complete contrast to my experiences at Sunday school when I was younger.

I followed the rest of those attending into the main room, and I did what everybody else was doing. I mean, I had no idea what I was doing, but I went along with the flow. I looked around at the large room, square in dimension and incredibly spacious.

The floor was littered with large cushions, and smaller ones. It seemed to have its own structure from what I could tell. I had no idea what to do, and I felt a feeling of self-consciousness slowly build up in my face. So, I just stealthily made my way to the back of the room and sat next to my friend.

The room grew silent, and then someone at the front of the room spoke and I heard what I thought was a chime. The audience started to close their eyes. So, I did the same. I started to think about what I'd got myself into.

I was sitting on this small cushion that barely supported my knees, and I could feel a slow ache ripple through them. I wanted to curse the moment when I'd agreed to come.

Then my flow of thoughts was interrupted by another ringing of the bell or chimes (I couldn't make up my mind which was which). So, I sat there and resigned myself to the long haul.

Despite my uncomfortable position, I was aware of this sound of pure silence. It felt eerie. What happened next was so confusing and disturbing that the only way to describe it was that my mind was trying to find a way out of the silence.

And as I sat in the silence, I could feel the room was starting to resonate with the silence within me; it was as though we were becoming aligned. We were becoming one. Then I felt this surge of energy ripple throughout my body, but especially from where my head was.

It was like being enveloped within an energy field that contained my whole body. Then this surge of energy moved out of my body, as though the force took the shape of a ball with a life of its own, moving at incredible speed across the room. It was as though it was trying to find a way out of the silence.

I was frozen still. Stuck. Physically unable to move. I was in shock. Then, after what felt like an eternity, I heard a loud and clear voice say, 'Count backwards to 10, slowly.' So, I did.

'10, 9, 8, 7,' at which point that part that I would later identify as being part of my mind flew right back into me, and we became fully integrated again as one.

As I continued to sit there in a complete and total state of shock, I really didn't know what to do. So, for the rest of the meditation session—which seemed to drag on forever—I kept myself busy by talking to myself.

I would like to say it was an incredible experience, but it wasn't. I didn't know what to think, feel or say. I had no experience or knowledge to describe or rationalise what had just taken place. The questions that came up later once I recovered were:

Who am I?
Followed by
What am I?

And then
What am I made of?
Then
Who and what was that voice?
And
Where had it come from?
Because I knew it wasn't mine.

When the meditation session ended, my friends and I left and headed straight to the pub. I desperately needed that drink. As we made our way down the escalator to catch the tube that evening, I couldn't help noticing that the amount of space and the depth of the angle of the escalator seemed to stretch for a vast distance.

It was as if time had slowed down and that space itself had expanded. What would normally have taken less than a minute to descend to the bottom seemed to take forever. Time and space were distorted. But I felt nothing, no fear; it's difficult to describe what is indescribable.

One day, I revisited the same station and remembered the experience of how the escalator seemed steep; whereas now the journey to the top was short.

When I eventually got home that evening after a couple of drinks, I sat down in the main room and I can remember a distinct and quiet soothing voice telling me:

You should get some sleep, you will be fine in the morning.

So, I did. I listened to that voice and went to sleep. When I woke up the next morning, I felt great and alive and continued to live my life, and the impact of the experience seemed to dissipate very quickly; in fact, so quickly that it was forgotten. I have had no memory of that moment or experience until now.

However, a month afterwards, I surprised myself by buying a book called *Zen Mind Beginner's Mind* by Shunryu Suzuki. I read a page a day, just quietly contemplating the information contained within, and I really enjoyed the read.

It was only when I got to the part of the book where the author writes that "Enlightenment is just to be yourself, your own true Buddha nature and there is nothing for you to do" that I remembered feeling anger and rage when reading the statement, which at such a moment would be considered to be out of character.

Back in Morocco, I stopped watching the repeat of that memory and the magnitude of what had once happened so long ago.

I sat there by myself in the quiet solitude of the mountain room, knowing that I wasn't ready to make that deeper connection, since the spiritual journey I was on needed to run to its own successful end.

My answers couldn't be found by reading a book, but by living fully as myself. This awakened one path had been set in motion a long time ago and I needed to have my own internal answers to that statement. I was just getting over the surprise that it was only nine years later that I was able to remember it.

Life or God, it would seem, wouldn't allow anyone or anything to interfere with the experience someone was having. In this case, it was me, having my own experiences and coming to the full realisation of my own inner understanding.

There was nothing wrong with that book, it just wasn't for me.

'Wow!' I suddenly felt.

Yes, it is, the voice said. *How do you feel?*

'I feel great,' I said, then it really dawned on me what had just taken place: I had woken up. I knew within myself that I was awake, truly awake. Spiritually awake. I started to remember even more. It was as though the dam had burst and the information from my life journey was continuing to update.

I looked up and spoke to the voice, 'Are you my guide?'

I was trying to put my finger on it; it was as though I had built, or better yet, I had designed the mechanics of what had just happened, as it felt so familiar and at the same time so surreal. It was as if I knew my own unique spiritual signature.

Somehow, at some level hidden deep within me, I was trying my best to remember exactly and precisely how I could have designed what had just happened, but I couldn't connect all the dots, not just yet.

Up until that point I had no real words from my own experiences to describe it, but it was like those times when you read an article or visit a place and it feels like you have been there or written the article yourself, which wasn't possible since you hadn't written it or visited the place itself; but it's exactly how you would write it, or you know the path and the way before you.

I continued to sit there and relaxed further into the experience. Then I realised that I couldn't hear my mind; it was as though someone had put it on a pause button, it wasn't there.

I had no mind. I knew that it was me, who was the thinker and that the thoughts came through me and then moved naturally to my mind. No wonder I couldn't pick up the subtly of distinguishing the me, or the I, the mind itself.

It, the mind that is, thinks it's me. The voice, or the presence and the sense of it, was still there. Then I realised I had been guided to this place. So at this precise moment in time, to wake up here in this room, on this day, year, right here and now was no fluke, it was intentional.

The voice was a part of the experience of reminding me who I am, what I am, and that the process of understanding the awakening had just begun.

I had had another eureka moment with the realisation that at each key moment from my past, when I had met key people on my life path, that had been intentional. This included the places where I had worked, the places where I had been, so that at the right time and at the right moment, I had everything that I needed to wake up.

All the experiences of my life were intentional, as the meaning in each one of them would assist me in my awakening experience. It had been planned all along, but with a level of perfection that I wasn't consciously aware of; it was operating through me, inside me and all around me, all at the same time.

I continued to sit there and take in the insight of the awakening and the sheer magnitude of what I now knew to be true. In each moment, my inner conscious awareness kept on expanding, with new knowledge providing me with insight. There was a sense of pure silence within me and outside of me. It was wonderful to experience.

Then I surprised myself by asking the voice again, *Are you my guide?*

It was as though the download had moved my understanding of life to a new level of awareness. I seemed to be searching for another question, but before I could ask, I was presented with an image of a floating, glowing yellow ball that seemed to hover right above a yellow brick road.

It was as though I was looking at a remnant of memories from films that I had seen as a child and a book that I had read many years ago when I was a teenager.

I'm rather more than that, my young friend but then again, so are you, the voice replied.

I knew that the voice and I were connected, so this time I asked, 'Are you the voice of my soul or God?'

I am you, becoming you, the voice replied. *You and I are becoming one: I in you and you in me. Welcome back and welcome home. What are you going to take up to the next base camp, and what are you going to leave behind?* The voice asked.

I laughed at the question, and responded with, 'What would you recommend?'

Well, let's have a look. You've packed an extra pair of boots. But let's be honest with each other, this is a hobby and a passion of yours, but this isn't your full-time vocation. Whereas for your host, he is the real deal.

He lives and breathes the mountains; this is his home; his office is the mountains. So, any gear that you are not currently or imminently using, you should offer to him.

On top of that, you have been blessed with the fruits of your labour. You could quite easily go out and re-buy virtually all your gear and it wouldn't hit your way of living. So, let's see what's in your bag.

I emptied out the bag and we went through each item one by one.

Are you ready?

I said yes.

How about any item that you won't be using or have duplicates back home? Offer them to him tomorrow and let's see what happens.

I found myself agreeing, and when I took a step back to look at what I was about to donate, I noticed that I had only about a quarter of my former possessions left. Yet, I had everything I needed for the duration of the trip to make the trek a success.

I felt happy with what I was about to do; no sense of loss at the amount of money I had spent over the years accumulating all this stuff. I felt lighter already.

It's time to get some sleep; busy day ahead tomorrow.

Trek to the French Refuge

When I woke up the next morning, I felt invigorated and alive. I could no longer hear the endless chatter of the mind, which I now realised had been running on in the background without really being consciously aware of it; it just seemed natural to me.

In any case, I would not have known how to distinguish that part of myself from the rest of me. It was as though someone had turned off the sound of a radio in the room and all I could hear was silence. I sat there, just enjoying the moment of solitude.

I checked the time on my phone, but I was around an hour early for breakfast, so I continued to lie in my warm sleeping bag and think about what had happened the night before. I still couldn't believe it.

I could focus on hearing the birds singing outside, as there was no sound coming from within me. It was great. I tested my leg, which felt great. I felt great. I just knew there and then that it was going to hold up in the mountains.

I was wondering how I could have completely forgotten the meditation episode at the Buddhist temple. It was quite incredible and surreal to receive all that information in one download at such a speed and in one go.

Decades upon decades of memories and experiences filling me up. I mean, who or what could do that? What force in nature, in life, could make that happen? It was a miracle of some sort and I still marvel at it to this day.

I decided to make my way outside and enjoy the sounds of nature. I nearly bounced out of the room with this new sense of energy, but I had to remind myself of my knee. So, I stood outside in the early hours and just drank in the sight before me.

It was beautiful. The colours seemed so much brighter, clearer and more vibrant, and there also seemed to be more space around, which I hadn't really noticed before. It was as though someone had come along and installed a wider-angle lens in my eyes and hadn't told me.

I continued to stare out and view the beautiful scenes in front of me and enjoy the sounds of nature and the vibrancy of the mountain valley. Wow! What a site and what an experience. I just sat there, enjoying it.

Then, I made my way to breakfast, which was as incredible as the dinner the night before. Knowing that I had a potential 4 to 6 hours walk ahead of me, I ate as much as I could.

Afterwards, I sat outside and drank the incredible Moroccan mint tea and continued to stare at the beautiful scenery.

I smiled at Mo, and he asked if I was ready. I nodded my head in response. Man, I was roaring to go. I'd never felt this kind of energy except in my early twenties. I had completely forgotten how that felt.

Age tends to creep up on you slowly without you realising it. It happens to all of us, the natural rhythm of life, and even more so when you are consumed with life's daily dramas, time simply flies by.

That morning I felt alive, and I could feel energy radiating throughout my entire being. I laughed as I remembered the scene from the film *The Sound of Music* where they all come down the mountain, singing—that's exactly how I felt.

I went back into my room and brought out the clothes that I wanted to donate. Mo's face lit up as he surveyed all the gear on offer, and within a couple of minutes, he was wearing the boots and a couple more items.

I felt better inside, and I noticed that any form of attachment to possessions that I might have had in the past wasn't present any more. I also knew he would make better use of them.

We made our way up the mountain path to our next destination, which would be the French Refuge that stood at 3209m; it would also be my base camp for the next three days.

It was warm for the time of year, especially at the base of the mountain, but as I looked around, I could see the wintry snow peaks in the distance.

I found myself enjoying the warm sunshine, and as we slowly made our way to one of the main mountain paths, I noticed that my guide was wearing a pair of shoes that I had donated.

As we continued walking on the path, I felt truly happy to be alive. Just to be here among the magnificence of the mountains was an incredible experience. I had forgotten what it was like to be so aware of my surroundings, and to enjoy the flow of life itself. It brought me a sense of peace and happiness.

Mo kept a relaxed and easy pace, which was easy to settle into, and I stopped every now and then to take in the sights around me.

You followed your own path, your own middle path, which had been laid out right in front of you in order for you to choose freely and openly, the voice said.

This was then followed by images from the previous night's download. I knew that what the voice said was true. I nodded my head as I contemplated what had just been said.

I continued to walk along the path, until just ahead of us, I notice a guy selling drinks and confectionary on the side of the path, right across from a waterfall. I thought it was a perfect place to stop and enjoy the sounds of flowing water. Mo offered me a drink and we both sat and sipped warm Moroccan tea. I smiled and thanked him.

It's interesting how people can change, the voice said. I quietly nodded in internal agreement.

I sat back on one of the chairs and slowly drank my tea and closed my eyes. I could hear the rushing water as it made its way downstream, and I found myself immersed in the natural sounds of the river.

Then it was time to move. I came back to the present moment, tea finished, and I relished the pace of making our way up the mountain trail, beginning our slow ascent to the next base camp.

The middle path. I'd never really thought of it that way until then, and only when I was aware of it. It's interesting that you can watch a film or hear a story but not make the connections with your own life journey.

I slowly took in the new knowledge that I was walking a path that was entirely of my own making, based on my choices. I became aware that the same was true of my interactions with life itself. Life had been a major player, a co-creator and the contributing factor to the experiences I was having.

All those people. All those events. All those situations. My life looked endless. It suddenly dawned on me that in order for me to tackle the bigger challenges in life, I needed to deal with the smaller ones first.

This was why I had met specific people, at a precise time and at particular events, so that I could have that exact experience, which would then lead me on to something bigger, grander, wiser, more fruitful and soul-fulfilling in the future.

It was like trying to eat the whole elephant at once; you can't, so you eat it piece by piece. Life seemed to work in the exact same way; you're being constantly stretched by being presented with small changes first, after which you can move on to something a little bit bigger, like moving up the ladder to the next level.

Also, I couldn't help but acknowledge that *living* in the moment meant one thing; but *being* in the moment meant another. To grasp the awareness and understanding of this realisation was profound.

We continued to make progress up the mountain path, and were soon greeted by the first evidence of snow. I was really enjoying the experience. I seemed to oscillate naturally from being at one with the environment outside me, and then moving back to the memories of the download inside me, without realising how I was doing this; but I was doing it naturally regardless. Maybe there was a divine helping hand leading me through the experience.

We stopped again at one of the small cafés, and this time, I paid for the round and sat, enjoying the small moment of relaxation. My knee was holding up well, and I noticed that the winter snow covered not only the valley on my left and right, but also the path in front of me.

Mo asked if I was enjoying the pace. I nodded my head and indicated that the Fanta was going down well. Then it was time to move.

I estimated we had another 3 hours to our destination, which would be the luxurious French base camp. On the previous two occasions, I had stayed at the 3-star version that was next door to it; but this time it was the 5-star accommodation, and I couldn't wait.

Did you notice that without the middle path you created for yourself, you wouldn't have been able to distinguish right from wrong?

What worked and what didn't work?

What were the areas of your life where you excelled by your own admission, and what were the areas where you didn't?

Also, when you made a wrong decision, did it still have a tendency to work out well for you in the long run? And were there times when you felt you had made the right decision, but it didn't go according to plan?

Did you also notice that even when you received the information or insight provided to you by your soul, there were times when you completely ignored it?

You couldn't help but notice that when you picked up the clues the first time round from your soul or life and acted on them without even thinking, it worked out better for you?

I took all this in as I continued to walk along the path and listened to the divine voice. I took in all the images, and the content and contextualisation that was contained within them and realised that it was true.

Not only were my experiences relative, but on each of the individual occasions, I could see how each part of my experience had played out. However, this time I was able to view it with objectivity, without any emotional attachments that I would have experienced if I was living it for real again.

I even noticed that when in the past, I had proverbially sat on the fence, waiting to decide or being indecisive, or when I wouldn't choose sides, or when I didn't fully commit to an idea that was when I had paid a price for it.

By the same token, without being fully committed or incisive during times in my life, how could I experience that part of myself without first gaining an insight from the experiences themselves?

It was like a reverse swing; now that I knew what it was like, I didn't have to choose that route or go through that pattern again.

As I went through these past images, I continued to gain new insights. I mentioned to the divine voice that it felt as if I was going deeper down the rabbit hole.

It's the opposite; you've come up the rabbit hole and now you're connected to life itself. I nodded my head in appreciation of the wisdom that had been spoken.

I soon found myself treading on snow. Mo was talking to another mountain guide, so I stopped and took a photo. I breathed in the cold mountain air and sipped from my water bladder.

I then brought myself back to view the images and the small films being generated to me via my mind. I could see moments from my past more clearly than when I wasn't aligned with other people on their path of life, and vice versa.

I would move off onto what could best be described as a new loop or movement, up or down to another level of life where the interactions would best suit me.

It was also like watching musical chairs; even when you thought you had 'lost' the movement, the dance of life would move you onto another layer or level of experience that was better suited to you and to others.

It was a never-ending process, one flowed naturally and effortlessly into another, in an experience that had no end; a system that was beyond the mind's understanding. I became aware that if you just viewed it from one side only, you might miss the entirety of the experience itself.

It was just that; only your own experience, but I now knew that life was running on a whole new level of spirituality that touched on everything and everyone all at once; a universal experience that had no end or even a beginning. It went on forever.

Success

I could tell that there were times when I had substituted my version of success for what culture or society had decreed from sources such as films, magazines, the media, etc. and even to a lesser point what my close friends' version was.

Interestingly, it never ever felt right when I followed these sources. I should have paid more attention to my feelings and to my own past successes.

I felt that I had become less grounded in how the world of life worked, and as a result had slowly faded due to a lack of acceptance of who and what I am, as me, in an attempt to appeal to other people's better nature rather than my own, and at times at the expense of myself, which had led to disastrous consequences on a personal level. I could see that quite clearly now.

Moving forward, I would now follow and decide on my own version of success and connect to the spiritual aspect of myself that was and is and will always be aligned to the ever-changing mosaic of life itself; to thyself be true.

The images moved again and were repositioned; so once again, I was getting used to the experience of it being like watching one small film clip followed by another. I noticed that there were consequences for each of those choices and decisions, and some were less obvious than others.

I really had been living freely and openly as me, with all my own ideas and beliefs, with my own internal understanding of how life works; also, to a greater or lesser point, I had accepted, as I grew older, the consequences of each of my actions.

However, what I had really lacked was the ability to grasp the impact of my actions on myself, and at times, also on others with whom I had interacted.

There had also been times when I had no, or little, control over events or circumstances. It seemed that at specific moments, my life just didn't really care about me; but now I knew that it did, because when it really comes down to it, it backs you to the hilt all the way.

You just really need to show up as you and have a little faith and belief that in the long run, it will work out for you. There are bigger mechanisms in the background at work, and it is not always just about you.

You must remember that you had everything that you ever needed in order for you to grow, including meeting the right people at the right moment in time, so that you along with others could share in an experience.

Lastly, life itself in all its shapes and forms has always been a constant factor in your life journey. There were times when you struggled to grasp some of life's lessons, because it's meant to be stretching.

It's meant to bring you out of your comfort zone, and that includes there being times when you're not always going to be successful. You will experience failure, rejection, fear, loss etc. That's life. That how it works for you and for everyone else.

What's interesting is when you let go of all your ideas and concepts about your understanding of how you think life is meant to work. Let go and observe; it will become very apparent how it really operates at all levels.

So, quieten your mind and let go; it's as easy as saying to yourself "let go" and watch the dance of life itself.

Then you will understand that just for that single moment in time, that's all that you ever really needed. The more you do this, your actual understanding of life itself will grow. It will become a perpetual motion experience.

I nodded my head in understanding; I couldn't help but realise that if you took each of those statements separately, the way in which you perceive the event or situation will determine your emotional sense of being.

I let go there and then, and felt the complete force of nature; I felt the expansiveness of the mountainside. I felt raw and wild.

Time passed and I continued to walk in the direction of the refuge. If I was having a hard time, it's because at some level I had created it, either by the choices and decisions I had made, or on some occasions by the opposite, by not making decisions.

Also, if I hadn't acted, it was due to many reasons; one of them being lacking confidence or belief in myself, and due to this, the places, the circumstances and the people I would meet but it was all intentional, so that I could grow as a human being.

Then again, I couldn't help but notice that this also meant that at times, life had been horrible and horrendous.

Well, you put yourself in each of those situations by your own design and at times by choice. You also said yes to allow others around you to have their own unique experience. It also depends on the position that you have chosen; this impacts on how you will experience life itself.

Also, the choice of words you used, the amount of work, energy and effort that you put in, will determine how quickly you can move out of those situations that you have put yourself into in the first place.

The best place to start is by acknowledging what is, rather than what isn't. That way, you can turn the levers of your internal driven experience, and in return, you can change how you experience life itself.

What is one of the favourite expressions in Africa?

'No pressure, no diamond,' I replied.

The voice said, 'Let's take a step back from this and take a breather.' So, I did.

I then breathed in the cold mountain air and noticed that I was starting to feel the effects of altitude. There came a gentle breeze of air, and I was again filled with the energy of life. I felt fully alive and invigorated. Wow! What a view.

We were nearly there, another half an hour to go, I thought to myself. I looked at my watch and realised we had been on the path for around 4 hours and were making great time. Twenty minutes later, we arrived at the refuge. It was totally incredible.

The French Refuge

As I stepped inside, I was greeted by the warmth of the building and a hot cup of tea. Looking around, it was very apparent that someone with love, care and attention had designed a fantastic place.

I crossed into the main room where trekkers retired after a day's festive activities. It was an incredible space. I just sat there recovering, and then Mo took me upstairs to show me where I would be sleeping for the next three days.

'Awesome,' I said as I dropped my gear. Then I headed back downstairs to sit in the chilled-out room. The room had a warm fireplace, where I sat down with fellow trekkers who were reading books, and just recovering from their climbs.

I closed my eyes and was just so happy to be alive. I had found Nirvana. No, forget that; not found but was experiencing Nirvana. I got it that heaven isn't a special place; it's here and now on earth, wherever you are; it's not a state of mind, it's simply a place of being within yourself where you can just be you.

I had found my magic spot in the universe; it was inside me all along. So, I just sat there in this complete immersion and experienced Nirvana.

Snakes and ladders, I heard the divine voice say, which was then followed by an image of the board game I had played when I was a kid. We all understood the concept that at all costs, you avoid the snakes on the board and try to climb the ladders, so that you can move up a level on the board as you go along.

You also roll the dice, since it's a game of chance and risk, while you make decisions and have fun at the same time. But it's a child's game, and I hadn't played it since I was a kid.

I could hear the voice in the background, *so, what do you think?*

I was again shown small fragments of my memories, which when repositioned and engineered into one clip of a film allowed the information contained within them to be re-engineered into a new framework.

This enabled me to have new insights and be able to relate to what snakes and ladders meant through my own internal experiences. As I watched, I noticed every decision made, every choice created, and every action I had followed through on; including the times when I proverbially sat on the fence.

But when I made the "right decision", I would move up via the ladder to another level and miss the snakes. When I got it wrong, I would be moved down a level. I realised that I had been a willing participant throughout the entire experience, and that I had agreed to this—not only with myself but with others.

Every action had consequences, some of them positive; so just as in the board game, there are rules that help you to move up levels—or like gears on a bike, move more easily—and have a more enjoyable time in life; or else, you may go down a level or two.

I was then shown an example of when I chose money for a role as a consultant without taking a step back and asking myself some fundamental questions; would the work in question move my career up a level and improve the quality of my personal life?

Such as when I decided to take a contract that took me away from London, and so missed the opportunity to continue to explore a new relationship I had started with this amazing woman.

As I quietly contemplated and reflected on what I had done to myself, I realised that I hadn't thought about my personal relationships, but more about my personal finances at the expense of everything else.

What was interesting was that the business contract came to an abrupt end, while interestingly what could have been the start of a fulfilling relationship also came to an end. Until that moment, I hadn't made the connection or realised the full implications of what I had done. So, I had moved down the ladder by quite a few levels.

I had been asking myself this question throughout my whole life journey, since I was a child. It was the type of question that I would ruminate over again and again, at the back of my mind. It was a simple question. I now knew that this was why I was on this life journey in the first place.

The question that I had asked myself repeatedly was, "What is really going on behind the grand curtain of life itself?" I mean, what is really going on? How does it work? Is there someone or something working wonders behind the scenes that we can't see, feel, hear or know consciously?

But we kind of know it's there. Or is something else going on that we are not privy to? I mean, how does it all work?

This was then followed by another sub-set of questions. "Why do some people succeed, and others fail? Is it meant to be that way? And is there some unseen force in the universe at play? Why are some people elevated higher in life, born with a silver spoon, etc.? Why had I such a struggle with a level of consistency throughout my life journey?"

Now I realised that it wasn't so much about understanding the rules of life; it was about understanding that they existed in the first place, and that they functioned perfectly well. It was I who needed to evolve and understand what every great master before me had done.

I should acknowledge first that they had existed, and then that they were there for a reason in the first place. Life wasn't just about me; it was about everyone else as well. I now knew that every one of us, each of us has their own individual challenges to navigate throughout life.

Some did it better than others, some by being more grounded in life itself; they get the message loud and clear and not only understand it but also use it to navigate upwards.

There was also a thing called Karma. I realised that it was true, but not as I had thought it was, nor was the understanding of what had been put into my mind of what it was and what it wasn't.

It wasn't as if I had previously believed in karma. The closet that I had ever come to correlating to Christianity was, 'To do unto others as others would do unto you.' What I understood it to be was cause and effect of oneself and my interactions with others.

You can choose to live consciously as the central point of the causal experience and feel its full effects on yourself by yourself or by others, depending on what role you've taken up in that experience.

Then, just as a pendulum swings from one side to the other, you and others can change roles; each feels the impact, depending on where you and they are in that moment and in the experience itself.

And it's real, the effect is and the residual can last for ages, not just in your mind, but in all parts of yourself; mind, body, and soul.

If you want to go up the ladder, then the thoughts, the words and the actions that follow can move you up a level by choosing to be a positive force in the world, by the actions that you take, the thoughts and ideas, along with the beliefs that you hold to be true.

The opposite is true; that you will move down a level if you have negative thoughts, actions and self-centred beliefs that only benefit you at the expense of others. When you cheat, you don't move anywhere; it's as though any forward momentum in your life diminishes, so you seem to stay exactly on the same path until you get it.

The issue with this that everybody else is moving on with their life while you are stuck in second gear. You also meet people at specific moments in time who you come to realise were once where you used to be, and vice versa; and it is due to this that you find it within yourself to be empathetic and compassionate, because you understand what it's like to be in their place.

I was then shown a memory of when I was on the receiving end of the effect of another behaviour. I remembered quite vividly what it was like to be used by a woman for the sole purpose of sex.

I can also distinctly remember hearing in the background what it was like to be a tool, for another one's pleasure. I initially thought it was I who was seducing a beautiful girl that my friend had introduced me to, but then I realised she never called me back after having months of fun together.

She had moved on to someone else, and came up with a fantastical story to tell me, i.e. that she was away on holiday. My friend broke it to me gently over a beer. So that is how it feels to be used for no other reason than for sexual gratification.

I remember that my ego took a massive hit; interestingly, I felt grounded for a week afterwards as I nursed my dented ego.

It also felt like I was living my life at different levels, or different aspects of my own being, like spinning plates, where in each of the individual areas or aspects of my being, I was either going up or down, taking the full benefits or effects of my life, sometimes getting it "right", and then at times getting it wrong; or my understanding of it was just that; mine and mine alone, but still having great results.

I remember when I was around 22 years old that I had moved completely out of my mind and connected to my soul. My soul asked me if I was on the right path to continue my degree, as I was now changing course from a humanities background to a business background.

Since I had no interest in becoming a teacher nor a lecturer at university, this change in direction felt right. Not only did I know at some instinctual level that it was right to change course, but also I knew that this was part of a plan.

I was just bringing it into being, here and now, and the reconnection to the soul was intended at this time and place.

It was also apparent to me that there were times when I would make that one single decision without bringing any level of awareness to it beforehand and thinking it through from beginning to end without even questioning if it was in my own best interest or that of others.

I was reminded again that *living* in the moment rather than *being* in the moment were worlds apart, and the two experiences differed hugely in magnitude.

Not only was I becoming aware that I hadn't paid much attention nor been fully conscious of the full implication, but there seemed to be the same repeating pattern throughout some of the small decisions that I made daily.

This included many of the same negative and destructive thoughts. I was completely immersed in the experiences that I was having. Good habits paid off and bad habits pulled me down. Karma was a bitch.

I just sat there, enjoying the natural rhythm of life as I slowly sipped my warm Moroccan mint tea. Looking out of the window, I could see how the winter snow had settled on the mountainside; it was a beautiful sight to behold.

I glanced at my watch; we had made good time, with dinner coming up around 6 pm. The effects of altitude were diminishing, and I closed my eyes to snatch a brief catnap.

A heartbeat, a small kind of video clip was presented to me, followed by another, until it became one clip interconnected with another. Then it was turned from its normal vertical position to become horizontal.

When I looked at what was being presented, I started to see image after image being presented, one over the previous one; and as I looked, I saw an image of the symbol of Ying and Yang.

The colours of the Ying and Yang were in the symbolic black and white colour, before being reversed back and forth, as if it was being held on a spindle; and as the spindle moved, so did the image.

I could feel within me that what was being conveyed was also about cause and effect. I kept my eyes closed and was presented with moments of my life. The focus this time seemed to be on when I had acted, rather than waited for things to happen.

I was then living as cause rather than as effect. I was also shown what it was like to be and to become proactive, rather than reactive. And there were other times I was feeling the effect not only of my decisions, but other people's, and the effect they'd had on my life.

I was shown an example of when I'd decided to create a solution for a company that I was working for, without having been asked. I could still feel the drive and the hunger and that sense of excitement that produced such a thrill when I finished a conceptual design for this new company.

Not only did I stay late in the office that night; I can distinctly remember feeling that time had no meaning, but the energy that moved through me in the creative experience raised me up to a whole new level of awareness.

I didn't even ask myself if what I was creating that day would work; I just knew that it would. When I came into work the next day, I eagerly presented it to the client, who intuitively knew that I had got it. It would capture and present the information required and was easy to use. He smiled and so did I.

I didn't have any real emotions as I was presented with this new recollection; I just had a better understanding of the life that I had been living.

As I came to, it was time for dinner. Man, was I famished. Dinner that evening consisted of lamb stew and the most unbelievable succulent bread, the kind that once you had one piece, you wanted another.

I found myself sitting at the dinner table with another solo traveller who had also decided to climb Mount Toubkal. As we made polite conversation, he told me that he had just walked across parts of the Sahara, and had visited the Mediterranean.

He wouldn't stop talking, and as I watched him, I noticed that he was living life on a high. What was apparent to me there in that moment was that here was a man who had found that special magic in his life, that piece of the puzzle.

It was as though he had decided to live life fully and was enjoying the moment of now. It wasn't that he didn't have a care in the world, it was something else. I could hear the voice in the background, telling me that he had embraced life and was at a place of *being*, rather than at a place of *doing*.

I think that before waking up myself, I would have considered the guy a little bit strange; I would have wondered about the implications of just setting off and going out into the world, to live on your own terms and travel by yourself.

But now I knew better, and I sat there, enjoying hearing stories from his life journey. We were more alike, and it was nice to be in the presence of another being who was living life to the full.

Mount Toubkal

I was woken up by a gentle nudge around the 5.30 am mark. Everyone else was fast asleep, oblivious, as I geared up for day one of the ascent up Mount Toubkal. This would be my third ascent, and I could feel the excitement building within me.

I had decided to wear multiple layers of clothing rather than one large jacket as I had found this to be cumbersome—especially when you're moving up at speed—and my body would be burning a couple of thousand calories per day. I didn't want that heavy, damp feeling of a large jacket weighing me down.

As we set off, I started to think about the climb and the challenges that lay ahead. I had always found that each trek presents a new challenge. On my first ascent, I was going into the unknown and had no idea what to expect.

The lessons from that experience were to become fitter, better prepared, do some research, reading about others successful endeavours.

On the second occasion, not only was I fitter but I was a part of a crew of six people who knew what they were doing, and we all had a great time.

This time, even though I wasn't as fit as I was before, I felt a sense of inner peace, and I just knew that I was going to be fine.

I layered up from head to foot, eager and excited by the prospect of a third and successful ascent. Crampons on, ice axe ready, gloves on, beanie on, zipped up to the top to trap the warm air, and a Gore-Tex jacket to keep out any form of external precipitation. Two pairs of socks and a neck warmer for a scarf. I was ready to go.

Mo appeared with a hot cup of Moroccan tea, which went down perfectly. I had found my relationship with Mo had been improving all the time; not only had I found him to be easy-going and a good laugh, but he really knew the mountains like the back of his hand.

He grew up at the foot of the mountains, and was a Berber by nature and by birth. He had a relaxed and informed manner as he knew the path we needed to follow.

Mount Toubkal is considered by many as a great introduction to Alpine trekking or climbing, considering your level of skill and expertise. What makes it so attractive is the fact that it's at altitude and is easy to get to from most parts of Europe.

At the top, it was one of the most beautiful mountainous regions that I have visited and attracted not only the most adventurous but also day-trippers who can make the 5-hour ascent to the refuge then turn back.

Plus, there is a spiritual temple at the lower end of the mountain that attracted visitors from throughout the world.

As we started the ascent, I found I was immersed in the pitch-black darkness of the early morning hours and my head torch lighting the path in front of me. I could feel the spikes on the bottom of my crampons gripping the snow as we slowly and methodically made our way up towards the mountain path.

Based on the experience of my previous trips of going up to Toubkal peak, I knew that there were large rocks and boulders ahead that we would need to traverse for the first hour, but going up had never really bothered me; it's coming down that always seemed to hold the bigger surprise.

As I looked ahead, I could see the multiple lights of other trekkers as they too meandered up and across the steep mountain path. *Poly-poly*, which means slowly-slowly, a phrase I was introduced to when trekking up Mount Kenya, had become my mantra.

As I reminded myself to manage the effects of high altitude on my body, I could hear Mo's voice as he said that we were making good progress.

I sipped from time to time from my warm hot water bottle; the temperature was around minus 7 degrees Celsius, and I could feel the warmth of the tea fill my body. We would soon leave the boulders behind and find ourselves on more level terrain, which steadily inclining its way upwards to the main peak.

I was presented with an old memory of myself when I was around 11 years old. I was sitting at the back of a bus coming back from an athletic event, when a girl sitting diagonally across from me turned and asked me a question.

I didn't hear the question she was asking me, but I can remember how I felt confused and incredibly self-conscious. I was at the age when girls were becoming a distraction for all the right reasons, and she was cute.

I didn't know what to make of the conversation at the time, but what I can recall is how her focus went away from me to another boy, and I remember how I felt, even more confused.

The conversation between the two of them continued and I started to recall what the theme was about. Then another girl joined in the conversation and so did I.

You're taking it in turns, the divine self observed.

Watch.

First, it was your turn, then it went back to her, then she moved it to another person, it became his, then her friend intervened and then you joined in.

I nodded my head, slowly understanding as I felt the information being brought up into my new level of awareness. It was as if the first girl had a large ball of energy that she had created when she engaged me in conversation; then she passed this imaginary ball to me in the form of a question.

I then passed it back to her with an answer, and so forth; we all moved this ball of energy around us, one to the other. The flow of energy accelerated when we were connected and contributing.

You always wanted to know what was really going on behind the scenes, behind the magician's door—the Wizard of Oz machine, as you call it. So, we are using this memory as a vehicle, to help you can understand this contextually.

You didn't know what to think at the time, but at a deeper and more complex level, this is what has been going on constantly throughout your entire life.

There is a deeper and underlying current of spiritual growth that's going on in the background of all your own individual actions, where each one of you is having an individual and then a collective experience.

Within this collective experience, not only are you are all sharing in the same event, but each single one of you is having your own individualised experience on various levels of reality; physical, mental and spiritual.

Most of your species weren't consciously aware of the spiritual aspect of the experience.

'I didn't think it was such a big thing; in fact, I had forgotten,' I replied.

Do you remember what you were thinking at that moment?

'I was wondering what was going on. I couldn't figure out what it was that she was asking me.'

You've given yourself the second answer; as you're not aware of what the other, or others, are thinking, it's not possible for you to really know that unless you ask; and even then, it's based on what that person is prepared to tell you.

Each one of you is sharing in the collective experience as equals, and that's why it works so well. Not only are all of you contributing, but each one of you is "getting" something out of the experience itself, that it is relative to each of you alone.

So overall in this scenario, each one of you is gaining insight and assisting you in forming your own unique outlook on life, including assumptions and beliefs, etc.

At that moment, I paused to take in the magnificence of my surroundings. I found that I was breathing quietly, due to the increase in altitude which plays havoc with your body. I was quite taken in by how beautiful everything was, especially where the snow had settled on the mountain range itself and added a whole new dimension of tones.

I was loving the sense of the mountain wildness, which was incredibly beautiful. It was still dark, but the dawn sunlight was just beginning to glow beyond the horizon.

'You mean, I tend to overthink things? I remember racking my mind for what was going on, as I had no idea.'

More than that, you were trying to figure out what was going on; and so you ended up spending all your time and energy on generating thoughts, but none of that was real, your thoughts i.e. they were just thoughts, but they felt real to you. The actual event was just that, an event, but your understanding and interpretation of it wasn't.

So, try not to get caught up with the endless flow of thoughts ruminating in your mind; they're just that, they're just thoughts, they're not real unless you decide that they are, but then don't be surprised in the real world when others don't share them. Let them go and move on. Are you ready to move on?

I nodded my head and set off to catch up with Mo as we progressed up the mountain.

I would later call this experience, closing loops or tying up loose ends from my past. Any question or open events from my past were to be investigated with the spiritual data included.

In turn, that part of my mind where data had been previously held was updated with new information. Any excess energy that I had stored or had previously unknowingly associated with the event itself was released and no longer running in the background of that part of my mind; it had been brought to the surface to be healed, released and let go.

As I kept moving up the path before me, I noticed that some parts of the experience were no longer looping around and latching onto other pieces of data with a similar theme.

Have you made a mistake?

As we progressed up the mountain, I could feel the ebb and flow of energy coursing through me. One moment I felt fine, but then a second later, I would feel deflated due to the lack of oxygen at altitude.

Based on my previous experience of trekking at higher altitude, I knew that this was to be expected and was part of the climb.

'Have you made a mistake?' I asked. 'I mean, by waking me up. There are people who have been serving God and devoting themselves to the service of others all their life. I remember hearing that it's known as a "calling".

'Some of them change their lives completely; they give up everything, all possessions, money, wealth, personal relationships in some cases and here I am, realising how significant this is, to wake up spiritually and reconnect consciously as one.'

I felt the quietness of my surroundings, with a sense of peace and calmness. But then the wind around me grew louder, and I could also see the bleakness of the mountainside.

What would best be described as an eruption of raw energy then came rushing up and through my entire being; I felt love, unconditional love, wave after wave of it, washing all over me, and with each of the waves of energy, I felt stronger.

I don't make mistakes, not at this level nor at any level. Everything in life happens for a reason, the voice continued. *You desired it and so did I. It has to be both of us; you accepted the invitation and so did I.*

An awakening and a calling are not the same thing; they are two separate, beautiful experiences and should be viewed as such, so try not to confuse them. A calling can be viewed as when God is asking that part of you to become a part of a greater experience.

A true spiritual awakening can be described as when the soul becomes aware of itself as a part of you, you become actualised, not just physically or mentally, but spiritually; and then the rest follows suit, which is what's going on now.

There is more to follow, young one. Allow the process to unfold naturally and effortlessly, and you will be delighted with the results. Trust me, I have done this on many occasions through the millennia. I really do know what I'm doing.

I was quiet as I took in the words, because I knew that they were the truth.

The people that you have mentioned, those who have chosen to serve God of their own free will and through their individual decisions, are fulfilled and rewarded in a way that is relative and fitting to them and to them alone.

In each single one of them, there is their own soul, which makes up a part of their divine self, and as they move through life, they are choosing, with the assistance of their divine self, their own chosen path, every single moment, and every single step of the way.

There are no flukes. It is by intention and divine design. There is a perfection that is beyond the human mind's comprehension and understanding.

There are those among you who have also chosen to serve God. They come from all backgrounds and walks of life, not just from monasteries or places of worship; they come in their own way, by their own thoughts, words, deeds and actions. That is their choice.

Love and respect, my young friend, love and respect their way, as I have respected yours, and they have respected mine. So just be yourself and allow others the opportunity, not that they need to ask you or anyone else for that matter, to be themselves.

Then you, my friend, will have the wonderful and rewarding experience of understanding what few human beings have ever truly understood; that there really is an underlying spiritual purpose to their work.

So, when they elevate and help others through the work that they have chosen, they in return are also elevated, but not at the expense of themselves or others. So be beautiful. Be loving. And be kind and considerate to others.

To make a conscious choice. Is that not a great gift? To choose and to know that you have chosen for yourself. As you have chosen, so too have they. Since it has worked perfectly well from your personal perspective, so too will it work perfectly well for them as well.

So have faith; there are forces in the universe that are hard at work and at play, working in you, through you and all around you and at times, as you. These forces have been there since the beginning of time and will be there until and after the end of time. This is known by some as the Alpha and the Omega; the beginning and the end.

I know that you do have faith; otherwise, we couldn't be having this conversation, it wouldn't be possible.

I continued climbing, probably now around the 3,800-metre mark. I started to realise with each question that I became more and more aware of these insights, and with this new sense of awareness, the wisdom contained within each moment was enabling me to grow within myself.

I stopped again to take in some cold mountain air. Wherever I looked, I saw deep layers of snow and the jagged rock face of the mountain above me. I continued slowly moving up the mountain, step by step.

You have found your own middle path, your own way through life, I could hear the divine voice say. *You have realised that you have chosen and made your own decisions. You wanted to know how it truly works; you used to yearn to know what was behind the magic curtain of life, and with people, and in turn yourself.*

This question or theme has been a driving force throughout your life journey, and you have spent endless hours, weeks, months, years, and decades, in quiet contemplation. It has endlessly fascinated you.

Why do people do what they do, and why do they change when it has been obvious to you that it's not in their own best interests or in others? I mean, it's so obvious, why can't they see it for what it is or was?

You once thought privately to yourself that this might be the work of God, which is interesting, because in some way, you are correct. However, your own understanding and your concept of "God" is just simply that; a concept used to describe the unknown and the unseen forces of life itself, including all the names and labels that have been attached to it.

You are also aware of the concept of what God is or was and still is, since its changes through the ages are based on the position that a part of humanity has taken for itself.

You will come to know this to be true, since you have woken up spiritually; and those who have not awoken in such a way would have figured it out for themselves, that humanity has been making it up from the beginning, best describing themselves as being given God's human form.

You couldn't for the love of you figure out what happens to people when they come to power. Why do they seem to transform into something else? You've been wondering privately to yourself what really happens to them when the curtain comes down and there is no one around. Why do they change?

Is it simply a case that they weren't telling the truth in the first place? Or do they put on a good show for others to get what they want because they realised that's how it really works? It's not ideal—it never was, nor will it ever be, it just simply is.

But more importantly, I know what was buried deep inside your own soul; it was what you truly desired to know, which was how does it really work for you as you and where is God in all of this? Does it or he or she really exist? Or what did they say once in that film, the Absentee Landlord?

You were looking from the outside, trying to figure it out, rather than coming from within and connecting as one with me. That's one of the reasons why we are having this communion, this remembrance, this reconnection. The returning of you coming back home to yourself and being as one.

My attention moved again as the spiritual energy washed over me. I felt alive.

As if with perfect timing, the sun came up and it was a welcome sight. Although I was moving in the shadow of the mountain itself, I felt incredible; any residue of what had just occurred had settled comfortably back inside me.

Mo then suggested we have a break, so I wolfed down one of my Mars bars and finished off the last of the warm tea. I looked up, and in the distance, I could make out a couple of walkers who must have been 200 to 300 metres in front of us, making their way to the top of Mount Imlil.

During my last two ascents of Mount Toubkal, I had found that the distance to the peak itself, was deceiving; it was further and longer than you thought, a bit of an optical illusion, especially with the route that most walkers took.

We took our time, walking slowly and just enjoying the moment. I knew that we were making great time and were on track for an early summit. We continued upwards.

We reached a point where I knew a steep climb began, before the mountain levelled off, which would provide a relief for the legs. Half an hour later, I found myself on the path that led straight to the mountain peak itself, and on to the end of the summit. I knew that I was going to make it, and quietly smiled to myself.

I looked to my left and saw the most beautiful landscape under the early sun's rays; it was a magnificent sight, the mountains blanketed with white snow and the hint of a gentle breeze.

I stood there for a couple of seconds, just drinking in the magnificence of it. It really was God's country, and I felt privileged just to be here and bear witness to it.

When I arrived at the summit, it was such a relief; a sense of euphoria rippled through me, and I just stood there, looking around. I was alive and in heaven. I blessed the moment and just took it all in at once.

The mountain marker, in the shape of a triangle, stood at the centre of the highest point on Mount Toubkal; surrounding it were stones, placed in a large circle. I sat down and refreshed myself with water and the food that Mo was offering, along with other refreshments.

It was so good to sit there, even though we would only be alone for a couple of minutes, because in the distance, I could see other walkers making their way to the top.

Wow! What a sight. I could make out a glimpse of the Sahara Desert in the distance. I noted that the desert was on my bucket list as a place I would like to travel across and explore. It was right up there with Everest base camp, and the Jordan trek.

It was beginning to warm up. I finished my drink, realising that it had taken us around 4 hours to get to the peak. *Not bad*, I remember thinking to myself, *not bad at all. Bring it on!*

I'd always found going up the hardest and coming down the easiest. Saying that, I had a couple of stumbles and slips, but you make up time, especially with the effects of altitude diminishing on the way down.

We started to descend at speed. Mo was relieved, as he let me know that he hadn't thought I would make it. He could have been right, except that since I had awoken up, I felt like a new man, and I could feel energy coursing through me. I felt like I was floating on air.

As we continued down, I suddenly slipped right onto my knee. Since the snow was a lot softer where I had landed, I felt no pain. I picked myself up and continued on down. Within 3 hours, we arrived back at the refuge, a total climbing time of 7and a half hours.

It was a great feeling. I couldn't help but smile as we made our way into the refuge, where a warm cup of tea was waiting and some small snacks. *Bring on dinner*, I thought, settling down in the warm main room and closing my eyes just to chill out. Mission accomplished!

The evening meal

I sat and watched the flames of the fire dance to their own rhythm and beat, enjoying the quiet sense of silence and solitude as I recovered from the day's activities. I was really relishing the moment and thinking that this was heaven, just to be still and in the moment.

My sensory acuity had expanded quite considerably over the last three days. Colours were brighter than before, and I seemed to be able to focus on each object quite clearly and absorb more deeply the environment I was in.

I started to think about my insights from the day's excursion, and came to realise that I had been walking my own middle path through my entire life; a yellow brick road, or my own golden path through the garden of life.

I had experienced the highs and the lows at every turn through the choices I had made and the decisions I had taken. Looking back now, I could see that I had literally, not just figuratively, made some fantastic decisions; quite a few in fact, and also some bad ones.

It was like looking at a heartbeat image of the pulse of the heart going up, then going down, and then continuing its natural rhythm.

Some of the best decisions I had made included quitting my job and going back to university to study. I'd known that I needed to upgrade my skill set, so I left behind a good career at the bank.

I was ambitious and driven, and on top of that, I had identified a long-time small niche in the marketplace, and rather than sit around thinking about it, I decided to do something active.

So I resigned, took out a student loan and joined the local university. It would be one of the best decisions I made. Within nine months, coursework completed, I received a call from an agent, offering me three times the amount I had been previously earning.

On top of that, I moved to London; a city that was thriving in its evolution, on the rise across Europe and the globe. Times were good.

I also remembered that I'd had a golden internal principle, which is that when it comes down to investing in anything, it is wiser to invest in yourself. So, I was in a great place; new city, friends, money and the lifestyle to go with it.

I also now remembered that I had been on a self-help course in London six months prior to my resignation, and I had written down my list of goals. When I was cleaning up my flat, I came across the list of goals. I remember reading each one, and noticed that I had succeeded in each endeavour. I remember smiling from ear to ear.

Looking at the bad decisions I had made, I knew when assessing them that in those moments of making them, I hadn't realised, or to put it more clearly, I had not fully been aware that they were bad decisions until afterwards.

Like when I moved back to the UK after living abroad. I was this young 21-year-old with no long-term plan except to visit; I didn't really show any initiative or ask others for advice on how to adjust to a new culture.

The first year was the hardest and the most demanding. I really needed to plan and prepare better and do more research on any long-term commitment. I'd been incredibly immature, and it came across. It wasn't the most successful year of my life, but the life lessons that I learned that year stood the test of time.

Now, looking at all with a new sense of clarity and certainty within myself, I realised that was life. If we all had a crystal ball and knew what was around the corner, we would all change our minds and seek perfection, rather than seeing perfection in the whole of it.

It's through making decisions that one realised what was good and bad; and that wisdom and knowledge was derived though undertaking the journey itself. That made me smile.

Sleep came easily that night, as I was looking forward to the trek down the mountain.

Coming down the mountain

I looked out and around one last time at the magnificence of the mountains. I made a small prayer of gratitude for what had taken place. It was now easy for me to believe in the power of recovery through love, and to acknowledge that a small miracle had taken place that would change me forever.

I had come to the mountains seeking refuge and solace from the life I had been living, from the place within myself that was exhausted and jaded; I'd been close to collapsing into an emotional burnt-out shell of a man.

I found myself fully and completely healed and loved from the inside out. I had been brought back to the land of the living. I was alive and well. I was no longer going to be a slave to my vices or fears.

I was no longer going to be driven by some unknown, endless need to be validated through all my achievements or accomplishments. Nor would I be driven by some sense that I needed to keep myself busy for the sake of being busy.

I was simply going to be myself; no magic recipe or ingredients needed, as I came perfectly gift-wrapped into this world as I was; all the magic of life and the universe already built within the fibre of my being and within my soul, just waiting to be realised and actualised in the experiences that I was creating for myself.

The body was the perfect vessel in which to experience myself as a human being. And the beautiful mind was perfect as it was.

As Mo and I made our way down the mountain, our conversation was in full flow; as on previous treks, there was nothing like an adventure to form a bond. Mo seemed happy to be making his way home, and I was just happy to be alive and well.

I had really enjoyed the last four days. I was looking forward to relaxing and enjoying my last day in the mountains, and I knew that I was ready to start living again; except this time I would be fully awake.

We made good speed, and within 4 hours, we arrived at Imlil, the place where I had first woken up. I said another prayer of gratitude, and looked forward to relaxing before leaving the next morning and making my way home to London. I slept in the exact same room, which was so welcoming, and enjoyed a deep, peaceful sleep.

Journey home

Before I made my way to the airport, I shook Mo's hand for the last time and thanked him for a fantastic adventure and a great time.

As I made my way to the plane, I found myself looking forward to going home. It had been such a long time since I had said that to myself. I felt the urge to bounce up the stairs of the plane, but I didn't.

I took my time instead. I knew that my life had fundamentally changed, not just from inside out; but I was also going to need to work on changing my physical form from the outside as well. My leg felt great, even with the fall when coming down, and I couldn't feel any tightness or twinges.

Through the spiritual awakening that had taken place over the past five days, I could feel the ripple effect throughout my entire being. I could now feel a sense of purpose flowing from within me, rather than coming to me from any external source.

I realised that moving forward, it would be I who would be creating and deciding what my sense of purpose was while moving through life, by being one with it; no longer thinking that I was separated from it, but now being a part of it.

On top of that, I would no longer be lost in my own thoughts, nor would I be preoccupied by the flow of images and stories that I had been reviewing from my past.

I hadn't really clicked that this had been going on in the background, because it felt so familiar; but in essence, it was really a smaller part of who I was in that specific moment, before I moved onto something else entirely.

I could now easily tell when the mind would subtly and gently move me into a slipstream of thoughts that it was generating, but now I naturally oscillated out of it. I now knew that the mind didn't know that it was my mind until I had woken up, since it had thought it was me and I it.

I realised that this was an easy mistake, since one of the many characteristic traits of the human mind is that there is small voice operating in the background of your headspace which tells you things such as past information that came initially from your own experiences and has been influenced by other external factors.

I no longer identified myself with my mind, since I knew that it was a part of me since my awakening, but not the whole of me.

Part Two: Back Home
a Clean Temple

As I arrived back home, I could feel the flow of inner energy vibrating throughout my entire being, and a sense of self-awareness and assurance combined with a calm confidence radiating throughout me.

It was the exact opposite of how I had felt when leaving my flat five days earlier. Then, I was ready to quit my job and take time out, so that I could regain my mojo and initiative and sleep. I mean, really sleep throughout the entire day and not care.

I was spiritually alive, which felt incredible. The emotional state that I'd been chasing for so long was now my natural state of being. Though I could feel my body was tired from the mountain walking, it was just wonderful to be free from the constant sound of chatter in the background of my mind; all was now quiet.

I paced slowly around each of the rooms in my flat, feeling a sense of spaciousness and freshness that was now becoming familiar. I knew that I had lived there too long; I had outgrown the place a couple of years earlier, but rather than move on and move up in the world, I had stayed. I shouldn't have.

I surveyed each of the rooms with a newer, calmer and clearer perspective; the place felt small and closed and lacked any real warmth. I felt out of place, and I wanted to move on. I realised that the rooms probably bore a close semblance to how I used to feel about myself and life in general.

I was open and ready for change and roaring to go. I could feel the drive, the hunger, combined with a spiritual energy of change. It dawned on me that I had grown too comfortable and had settled into this life for far too long.

My friend once said to me that awareness is curative, he was spot on. I was also acknowledging that my spiritual side had presented me with countless ideas, but I had abandoned the spiritual path by ignoring any new insights presented to me, and by negating or rationalising with myself.

I had endlessly come up with excuses for not believing that anything was achievable in the first place, even when all the evidence around me in the real world of life was telling me otherwise. The decision not to move out of my flat was a great example of this.

I felt no anger, nor any sense of loss, just a sense of closure.

You couldn't see it for what it was but now you can, I heard the divine voice say, followed by, *you should have moved years ago, but you decided to stay; even when presented with ample reasons to move on, you stayed regardless.*

'I agree.'

Are you ready for real change?

'Yes.'

Because we start tomorrow, so get some rest as you're going to need it.

The dawn of a new era

Early the next morning, I woke to the sound of a voice that could have been the drill sergeant from the film *Full Metal Jacket, Move it, move it, let's go, go, go, go.* It was so loud reverberating inside my head that I literally fell out of bed.

I looked at my watch and saw it was 6 am but I knew I needed to make changes, so I got out of my flat, ready to go. I had used my injury as an excuse, when there were so many other ways to keep in shape, but I had become lazy, and I knew it. So, no more bullshit excuses.

On top of that, I was feeling great about myself and life in general. I needed to show my love and respect for my body, and have greater respect for myself.

I had to raise my standards, as I couldn't help noticing that every time I acknowledged and spoke the truth, there came a form of acceptance, which resulted in a surge of energy moving up inside me.

So, I was out of the flat on a cold January winter's day, heading in the direction of the Thames Path tunnel crossing. It was freezing.

Clean living also means clean eating, I heard the voice say.

I pulled my beany down lower, pulled my gloves up, and tried not to notice that there wasn't anyone else on the path that morning. It was just me, the seagulls, the waves from the River Thames, and the bitter wind. I couldn't help but smile to myself. I wouldn't take the risk just yet with the right leg, but I could still walk.

You have realised that the way you view yourself extends into the outside world, and there is no better way of seeing evidence of this than by looking at how you treat your physical form. So, rather than keeping on telling yourself specific and negative stories, you should change them and make them more uplifting.

Not only does this have the power to have a positive impact on your mental state of being, but it can also assist you to transform your body in a healthy way.

It will take time, hard work, commitment and lots of love and attention. Loving your mind means healing the body. Loving your soul means loving yourself and the whole of life itself.

Loving all of yourself as one total being means acceptance as one with the whole of life itself. Total acceptance of what is.

I stopped and looked at the flow of waves as they moved across and became one with the river. I could sense the winter chill as I breathed in the frosty air, but I also felt elevated by these words.

Love wasn't a word I used that much, in fact it was rare. I would usually use the word "like", another form and way of negating.

I see that you have started slowly putting it together, I heard the voice say.

I nodded my head in agreement. The sound of the water was infinitely soothing.

Within a couple of minutes, I arrived at the park across the river on the side of Canary Wharf, at the start of the Greenwich tunnel. I took in the immense stature of the large trees as I walked past them.

They were huge; I hadn't really noticed that before, how big they were. I had been in this park many times over the years, but now I was seeing them with a sense of newness and freshness. I could feel an inner peace and quietness within me from the awe and magnificence of them.

I took my time and it's an interesting thing, time; you think it's linear, but it isn't. It sometimes has a tendency to slow down and release its hold on you.

I sat down on a log and closed my eyes, embracing the quietness and the calmness of the moment. I allowed it to just wash over me. Any tiredness or fatigue I may have felt from being awake so early in the morning was gone and replaced by a sense of peace and belonging as one with life.

I looked across at Greenwich Park on the other side of the river, marvelling at the view, as if it was new. I laughed and smiled. A dog walker saw me and smiled and continued her way. A couple more minutes passed.

Would you like some tea? The voice said.

'I would love a cup.'

There's a coffee shop over the other side of the river. It's on me.

That made me laugh, as I headed in the direction of the coffee shop via the tunnel. I tried to remind myself when was the last time I had been there. It must have been over a year.

Within a couple of minutes, I was sitting down, enjoying a warm cup of tea. It went down well, and it was nice to catch my breath. I just sat there, enjoying the quiet solitude of the moment, till I decided, 'Time to go.'

As I made my way off, I took in the impressive view of the skyscrapers around Canary Wharf, which seemed to stretch to the heavens. The whole area of the city reminded me of what I had achieved and what I had given up just to work and eventually live here.

I also remembered studying ancient civilisations; how Cairo stood as a centre of civilisation thousands of years ago, strategically situated on the Nile, with its Pharaohs supported by the flow of financial wealth, just like London now, one of the great financial capitals of the world. The same features seem to repeat itself through time.

Who would have thought that a kid whose parents were originally from working-class backgrounds, who had also worked their way up to being successful, would one day have one of their sons working in an Emerald Isle tower of financial wealth? Not bad, not bad at all.

You earned your money the hard way, I heard the voice say.

'What do you mean?'

You worked for it, you earned it, it's yours, let no man or women say other. You didn't cheat or steal, but through hard work, you made a place for yourself.

This is the best way, as you come from a place of having no doubt; nor would you need to question how you accumulated your money; there is no doubt of its validity. This is the best way, to bear fruit that is nourishing for the soul and the mind and the body. Shall we move on?

So, I did.

The walk back was enjoyable. I relished the quiet solitude of the morning and witnessed the dance of life around me. The river flowed onward, birds floated above and around the waves searching for food, and another guy was taking his morning walk.

As I made my way home, I contemplated what had been said; it was great news, and it was great to hear it. I now looked forward to my next stage of growth and development.

Embracing the new

As I went through each of the rooms in my flat, I took mental notes on all the possessions that I had acquired.

On one of the bookshelves, I saw row upon row of DVDs and books, some that I had never got around to reading and had kept around for a rainy day; they would have to go.

I also noticed a small bookcase I had put together myself, not really knowing what I was doing but which seemed to defy the laws of physics by standing there, perfectly balanced and still.

That would also have to go. This made me smile, but I knew in my hearts of hearts that I had to let it go. Whereas the larger bookcase that stood on the other side of the room could stay, but all the books, CDs and DVDs would need new homes.

I knew in a gentle and caring way that my decline, which in turn resulted in me losing my edge in life and to a greater extent, the decline of my mojo, had started a long time ago.

My lack of awareness of the lifestyle that I had been living and the subtle but accumulated impact on my personal well-being had gone on in the background unnoticed by me, as I had become so self-absorbed in my daily living.

I really should have taken time out of my life and had a sabbatical, but I was too busy chasing the rainbow; a colourful metaphor that I use as one of my personal stories, telling myself that I was never really satisfied with the life I was living and was always looking for the next best thing, hoping that I wouldn't miss out on anything.

I'd been living in the moment, literally, without a long-term plan or vision to move me forward to new heights, or a dream that I'd find so fulfilling that it would make all the effort worthwhile.

I'd had no idea that my soul ached for fulfilment, a loving connection with me. 'If you don't go within, you go without.' Whoever said that had never spoken truer words. It meant a connection with God, on a conscious level or even on an unconscious level.

I'd gone out into the world seeking answers and hoping to find happiness and success in all my endeavours, in all my crazy shit, but not really getting the message. I'd never really stopped to contemplate and ask bigger, better and more soul-fulfilling questions.

But now I knew, now I had answers, now I knew what inner peace felt like. Now I knew what I had been up to, knew I could just simply be me—what a revelation! Simple words, yet so hard to experience; a revelation you couldn't buy—just simply to be yourself.

As I started to look at my clothes, I realised they would no longer fit me. It wasn't just that they were out of date, even for the old image that I had of myself before going to Morocco.

I could see that I had also been out of touch with life in general, not only for my age but also my economic status.

I sat down and just took it all in. I even noticed that some of my possessions were remnants of ideas that I'd had of myself in my 20s, and I should have moved them on.

I decided there and then on a key principle that I still practise to this day; that if I don't use one of my possessions for more than a year, barring seasonal variations, I will pass it on to a new owner.

I really had lost my edge. Wow! If I had been told this truth before "waking up", I would have been devastated by the news, but now I just acknowledged the truth of it.

I acknowledged to myself there and then that I hadn't been making the small incremental decisions that I needed to make, by stepping up in life when I needed to for myself, and moving my focus, my energy, my thoughts, by telling myself more uplifting stories, disengaging any negative beliefs and replacing them with tangible, measurable ones and then engaging with life itself, the true teacher of us all.

One of those negative beliefs, which became one of my all-time favourites, was waiting for the perfect moment or the right time to act. Screw that, I needed to get on with living life and allowing it to show up as it is, not as how I would like it to be.

I had moved beyond the mind and embraced the present moment; this is where life really is, the here and now moment, and I would now operate as much as I could by being there and by being present.

I now knew that I was a co-creator of my life journey, and life itself would, and had, and will continue to move me to the right place regardless. Just let go and allow it to happen.

Are you ready? The voice called out. *You're going to need some black bin bags. Let's start with the main wardrobe. Okay, you seem to have a fixation with the colour blue. You should be aware that there are many colours in the rainbow, and blue is just one of them.*

Anyway, moving forward; that jacket you wore just once and never again, in fact you never liked it, you should have taken it back, or better yet, used the return service. Let's pass that one onto someone who will make better use of it.

*Now, as we move it on, I want you to say the words, **"I release you"**.*

So, I did, and with each item that I moved on to a new life and said the words, I felt the energy within me change; I felt a little bit lighter each time I did it.

Secondly, I want you to say, "Thank you". So, it's now "I release you and thank you".

I found that each time I moved on a piece of clothing, the state of my energy changed; it went up and up.

Within a couple of hours, I had filled up more than ten bags of clothes, and I only had a few items left hanging in my wardrobe. I stood back and smiled. I was becoming clearer and clearer in myself, and the energy within me was bubbling to the surface.

Within a week, I had moved around 80%—okay, around 90% of all my possessions on to new owners. Not only did I feel better inside myself, but I wondered if it had been I who was wearing my clothes, or did they wear me?

With each daily change, I felt the surges in my energy increase and the level of awareness within myself expand. I also continued experiencing moments of pure silence, which would last for hours—or sometimes minutes.

Not only did I find the experience to be refreshing and reinvigorating, but it was as though someone had turned up the volume of the external world around me. The sound was incredible.

European travels

Next major event, I was arriving easily and effortlessly through the airport of Bucharest. It was a cold winter's day, and as I left the airport, I was greeted by snow, which made me smile. I had been noticing lately that I didn't need many reasons to smile and laugh; it just happened.

I took a taxi to the hotel, and the driver kindly started offering me the deluxe services of a local strip joint. I politely declined, but thanked him nevertheless, which also made me smile.

He then advised me what I would be missing, and as he drove with one hand on the wheel and the other on his phone, he showed me a quick video of the girl in question and what I would be missing.

I still declined, but I did admit the lady looked great. We both laughed as I got out of the vehicle and made my way to the hotel foyer. I realised I was in a great mood.

How do you feel about tomorrow?

'I feel great; if anything, relaxed and ready to go,' I responded.

Are you up for a conversation, because I would like to discuss something with you that will make it a little bit easier tomorrow?

'Sure,' I replied.

In tomorrow's session, just be present. This is going to be an enjoyable and exciting year for you, and you will be surprised how much you have changed. You will continue to change and to evolve. The external world in which you reside has not, but your understanding of it has.

You will continue to experience the associations of feeling more awake, more aware, more present, and more naturally you. This will present its own challenges. So, relax into the experience and just be you.

As you become more and more aware, you will notice that being you works perfectly well all the time. No need to be anything you are not. You knew this conceptually, but now you know that this is true for you and for others.

Concepts will no longer hold their sway over you. You will only be interested in what you're experiencing in the moment of now. When you're dealing with other human beings, you will be reminded continuously who and what you are in that moment, real-time, not the fabrication of the mind time.

You will also notice the implications of your own choices. So, be yourself and allow others to be themselves. It worked perfectly well for you, and you came home. We are one, you and I. If you allow the path beneath you to unfold naturally, then the experience that you are having will be and become natural and relative to you—and to you alone.

So too for others, because it is for them as it is for you; the only difference is that you are awake and aware of this on a conscious level, while they walk their path on a unconscious level. So, let's get ready for work.

The next few days flew past as I found my work becoming more and more enjoyable, which made my days fly past and I felt refreshed by the work I had been doing.

When I returned home at the end of the week, and as I continued to look over my place, I knew that there was more work to be done.

A new routine

Would you like to make your life easier? The divine voice asked, to which I agreed.

Well, let's begin. Please close your eyes, it said. So, I did.

I was then shown all the activities I had done throughout the day, literally hour by hour, and my interactions with others. It was like watching a video of the day and how it unfolded.

As I watched, I noticed very clearly what I was doing, saying, behaving and being, including my thoughts. Going through each of the interactions, I was reminded of the spiritual aspects of the exchanges that I had so far experienced since my awakening.

During each of the hourly segments, I not only acknowledged what I actually did, thought, said and how I behaved, but with the awareness itself, I realised that I could make small and subtle changes, so I did. It was like a 24-hour cycle event.

I noticed that I had become more considerate to others and to myself, which made a world of difference. It was as if doors that had been previously closed in a room were now wide open, bringing in air and a new sense of life.

I would also remind myself not to focus exclusively on my own needs and desires during the day, but to let go of any expectations that I might have and let life in. This really freed me up to experience more of life.

I found that after each session, the space and quietness would reverberate in my evening meditation sessions. Not only did my meditation sessions became longer and deeper, but the outside world and I become naturally as one.

I also noticed that if I went too deep into the mediation session, I would be awake for hours afterwards. Although it was beautiful, I needed my sleep. I was still new to this, and I laughed at the *hitches* in my progress in a natural and healthy way.

Part Three: Trials and Tribulations

February

I could still feel the effects of the cold weather as I looked across the Thames. But the sound of flowing water was soothing and relaxing.

I was slowly getting used to being woken up in the early hours of the morning, and was seeing the dramatic results of becoming physically lighter and fitter. The benefits of regaining control of my health far outweighed any sense of discomfort I felt at the beginning of the day.

'What if I don't continue with my current way of work?' I asked

I'm surprised you ask; your work has been assisting others, and in the process, it has helped you earn a living. You have no residual value since your intentions are clear, positive and sound.

You have no hidden agenda, no hook-ups, no karma to repay, no open loops to close. You've been working through them. You've been clearing out your mind, making it into a clean temple. You have paid your dues.

I took all this in and quietly contemplated what had just been discussed. I closed my eyes and meditated. Days were becoming weeks and I soon found myself just enjoying life.

Panic attack

Then one day, I woke up and started to panic. It felt like the ground beneath me had been pulled away and I was in free fall. I had no control and was completely helpless.

I hated this feeling. As a man, I felt completely disarmed, emasculated. It was horrible. I can't ever recall having a panic attack in my adult life, only going back to my pre-teens, if not even earlier. Wow! What a horrible feeling.

Then the feeling subsided. It was Saturday and it was my day off, my time.

Do you want to talk about it?

'No.'

Keep the faith. If you didn't have any, you wouldn't have woken up. Keep the belief. Because if you didn't have any, you wouldn't have woken up.

Keep the confidence in the you and the me. If you didn't have any, we wouldn't be having this conversation. Let go of what just happened and let's move on.

This is a part of the process. Have faith, because I know what I'm doing, letting go isn't easy when you have little experience in it. It's like a muscle; when you first start, it's difficult; but as you put your time and energy into it, it gets easier, and easier, and over time, it will become a natural part of your being—because it is.

Have faith, continue to believe in yourself, you've come so far, let's keep on going.

I was out of the flat and making my way along the path to Greenwich.

I let go again and felt all my emotions drop and drift away, and then I felt the energy of my soul fill me up. I was fine and calm again, the awareness of the moment washed over me, and my focus switched to the external world, with the previous moment completely gone.

I was feeling stable, solid, grounded, and calmness spread throughout my entire body.

Natural relationships

Are you ready? I have something I would like to tell you, and there is no other way to say this. I nodded my head as I continued my walk.

It was still cold, but you could see signs that we were halfway through winter. The natural laws of a UK winter are dark cold mornings and cold winter evenings and nights.

Over time, I was becoming fitter, which resulted in my walks becoming longer, and I had to challenge myself. Along with that, my knee was completely healed. Time was a great leveller.

You've never really had a natural relationship in your life. The closest ever was with your parents.

Wow! The statement stopped me in my tracks, and I felt my energy drop down to the bottom of my being. 'What about my brothers?' I asked.

Normal sibling rivalry means love and its opposite, and there are times when you have displayed these natural tendencies. Your relationships with the two of them have normal and natural characteristic traits.

Please notice that I use the word "natural" and not "normal" as they aren't the same, but the two are easily distinguishable from each other.

Normal is a word that was created by people to explain how life works based on how they think it should work according to standards and expectations that they set for themselves and at times for others. In some cases, more for others than themselves.

Thus, the statement "is the norm" springs to mind. You hear people say all the time that they want to meet a normal person. They're looking for a normal relationship.

But "natural" is usually associated with the forces of nature and is not derived from human beings, even though being human is also a natural force of life and nature.

Except you all seem to believe that you are excluded, since you are a conscious being made in the image of God, and thus some of the basic natural foundations blocks of the universe don't apply.

This is also true but then again, since God resides in all things, then your relationship with the divine tends to be normal rather than natural. Stick to having a natural relationship with yourself, then God, then life and others and you will have more success in life. This is how you can live in perfect alignment.

People rarely say that they would like to have a natural relationship. Your relationships, and what I really mean here is your personal relationships with people along with intimate relationships, are close to normal. There are trade-offs, and most of your species have come to realise that this is true.

You need a level of practicality in your relationships in order for them to work. A level of maturity is needed from all sides of the paradigm, including yourself. In fact, I would say more from you, since you now realise how it really works.

Most people will unfortunately go to other sources, under the impression that what they are reading is true, at the expense of their own personal experiences and spiritual side. This is a great shame, the greatest of human tragedies.

When in doubt, my young friend, you will always find me in the silence. You will always find me if you truly seek to know and experience the answers that life has to offer. That is why I am overjoyed that you accepted the invitation to "wake up".

This is an invitation to all people, not just the select few; I'm not an elitist, or prejudiced, or racist or sexist, since I have no ego, wants or desires.

Let's make sure that what has been written in my name by others wasn't, and isn't, nor will ever be a true substitute for the real divine connection. Most of the stories that are in your religious texts are a human attempt to understand the unobtainable.

It's not possible to contain the magnificence and grandeur of the divine in a holy text. Divinity can only be truly experienced, not written or spoken about; and on top of that, I would also like to have the opportunity to represent myself.

I don't really need an intermediary, unless you all consider yourself one, and even then that would include your entire species.

I can see and feel that you're in shock. The cruelty here is that if you continued to believe in something that had never really existed, except in the fabrication of stories that you've been told by "others", including your religions or the media, or better yet, by other so-called experts who themselves don't even live the lifestyle they are promoting, because they put business before honesty, then that is that.

You will continue to believe in something that never was or was never real in the first place. Wouldn't it be easier just to be told? Since this is a holy work that you and I have embarked on, a fabrication of your beliefs and narratives in your mind will no longer suffice. It's easy to tell you that I do this out of love, not out of cruelty.

One of the stories you were told from the Christian Bible is that I have only one son, and he died for the whole of humanity. This isn't true. As we speak, I have billions of sons and daughters from all different backgrounds, different races, beliefs, sexuality, not just one.

Plus, what was interesting was that when Jesus told his followers and disciples "that ye are gods", he was spot on, so they don't need to be saved. They are all your family, all of you.

How about that for an answer? I don't play small, it's not my style, because I play at all levels, big and small, that way I can't lose. I always win.

If you really think about it, since I reside in every part of life itself, there isn't any position or angle from which I couldn't see that part of myself interacting with another part of myself.

So, I interact at all levels with all parts of my entire being. By the way, I'm using your words, your concepts contained in your mental storage and imagery when having this dialogue.

If you had studied maths, science, or philosophy, I would have used words and concepts from that data contained within your mind; I would just have approached it from a different perspective.

I love the fact that in some parts of the world, I'm an artist expressing myself, and in other parts, I'm a scientist trying to figure out what the other part of the universal life experience has been up to.

Man, I really am in everything, everywhere and in all and I am so much more than you could ever imagine!

I nodded my head.

A natural relationship with yourself and others must be based on pure honesty first. You're under no obligation to inform another unless you choose to speak your truth as you know it to be.

When you align your truth with the natural laws of life—and what is meant by this is that natural relationships are meant to serve a divine purpose—then truth frees you up to be yourself.

It opens your mind to all possibilities and opportunities. Normal relationships tend to have an agenda, which can roughly translate into "what's in it for me and for me alone"; you usually only consider the other person afterwards, usually when you've got what you wanted.

This has the characteristic traits of a business deal, or a business relationship. There seems to be a level of pragmatism to it; or better yet, there is an honesty that is not being openly expressed between the two of you.

You and other human beings are trying, to the best of your ability, to have a natural relationship. But until you do the inner work, so that it is then reflected in the outer world, you will continue to struggle.

While you are figuring out what's best for you, you make mistakes; which is also a part of the life journey. Through your own experience, you would have noticed that as you became older and wiser, you generally start putting things into the right place and in the right order, as long as you don't allow your ego to get in the way. It's challenging, it's meant to be, otherwise you would have no appreciation of it.

Most people find it easier to manage their work life instead of their personal life, since they are dealing with one of the most complex and complicated beings on the planet; another human being, who has his or her own needs, desires, insecurities, expectations, etc.

That why it's so difficult. In school, you don't discuss personal relationships, sex, or other key areas, as it's seen to be the domain of the parent or religious figures. This is a major flaw in your species' thinking.

School combined with the collective wisdom, intelligence and experience of the elders should provide a solid and honest foundation for your youth, so that you can all grow and benefit from others experience, not just your own.

You do this with science, maths, and any scientific and analytical path, but not the most important areas of what it is to be a natural human being with all your emotions.

'So we *are* a collective,' I suggested.

You've always been a collective, in more ways than one. You're a collective within your own species. You're a collective of individual beings or souls that are connected and interconnected at all levels within the living experience of life itself.

But you are separate at the same time, by purpose and by design; by the design of your physical form; but even then, you are still connected.

If you took away all your products and services, you would notice that every one of you is in some way servicing another; this is also by design, you really are interconnected.

No man or person is an island. You each create your own unique individual experience by design, and include others in the experience. When you do this, it is so each one of you can experience something that is relative to them and relative to others.

This experience is added naturally to the greater and collective experience of your species as a whole. That is why the statement "We are One" resonates with truth.

You are also connected to your planet, and it is also connected to you. Earthling. You are also part of the spiritual collective of the universe, the cosmos in your mythology. You would or have or may call this God, or by any other name that you would like to associate with religiously.

Then you could also say "We are One" with your own species; with the planet and all its life forms; one with life; and one with God. Or take away the name or label of God and put in your own religious name, and it would also be the truth as you know it to be. Isn't that wonderful?

Now that your contextual understanding has been expanded, based on the information above and repositioned, it will be easier to proceed to the next level up, to enable you to delve into a more in-depth understanding of how your interactions with life, the planet, others, and the universal forces of life work, and even your understanding of the concept of a single deity, God.

You will no longer need to see the world just through the lens of your own chosen words or the context in which you use your mind to filter incoming data. You can now, if you

*choose at any given moment—in the here and now moment—
use the fullest extent your mind, body and soul as one.*

*Words are just words, so make sure you that you select
the ones that suit best in any given situation; and if that
doesn't work, drop the words, come back to the present, here
and now moment, and from within this new space select again.*

Relationships

Watch, do you remember, do you recall?

Then the voice played me a scene from many years ago in
my past, when I was sitting on the sofa and channel hopping
until I came across the film of *Dorian Gray*. I remember being
morbidly fascinated by the character and repulsed at the same
time.

I remembered exactly how I felt, except that this time as I
watched myself watching the film from an observer's point of
view, it made a world of difference.

I was transfixed by that main character in the film, who I
really despised as he descended further into his decline and
those experiences he was having at the expense of others and
in the end of himself.

I could now see and recognise some of my own
narcissistic behaviour when I interacted with other people. I
distinctly remember times when I was solely focused on my
own self-gain even at the expense of others, and I could now
see how I fed off my friends' energy and how they fed off
mine.

I could also now see some of my relationships with
women for what they once were. Some of my experiences on

the intimate level were at times incredible, as we both enjoyed and got what we wanted from our interactions.

If it's any consolation, you met your own basic needs, wants and desires. They said yes and so did you. You adorned yourself with friends who told you what you wanted to hear and say, and by the same token, so did you.

Most of the time, it was harmless fun, but somewhere along the line, the Peter Pan complex had to be shed, or better yet grown out of. You should have let go, evolved and matured into something wiser and more balanced, was the obvious message. But you simply ignored it, despite being repeatedly told over the years.

I'm glad that you picked up the vital clue here. The interesting thing is that life did show up at the right time and at that right moment, so that you could watch the perfect film to inform you or provide an update on where you really were on your journey through life. Please don't let the fact escape you that the timing was perfect, don't deny it.

You couldn't figure out what was happening to you, and yet somehow, quite a few of your friends made better decisions and evolved out of their relationships.

Is it fair to say that you had seriously underestimated the implications of your own chosen lifestyle, and this rippled and impacted on every other area of your life?

Isn't it interesting that when you step out of your own mind and evaluate it with a clearer and fresher perspective without any emotional attachments or judgements, then it becomes easier for you to evaluate it for what it was?

For where you really are? And as importantly, if it no longer serves its purpose, then you choose or create a new path.

'Tell me,' I asked, 'how was I meant to know that? I mean, how was I meant to make the connection?'

You have been reminded on more than one occasion, in fact on so many that it's unbelievable that you chose to ignore it repeatedly. The choices and your own decisions are yours and yours alone, the voice reprimanded me.

I was shown the same message conveyed in many different areas of my life; then I knew that I was being told and shown the truth of my ways. I could see it clearly for what it was, and acknowledge it for what it was. It was a really sobering feeling.

'Yes, you're right,' I said.

Then with this acknowledgement, new insight and wisdom flooded through me; I knew that I wasn't a horrible person by any stretch of the imagination, but like the character in the film, I was acknowledging my previous lack of accountability and responsibility for my own actions, and not having considered the effect of my actions on others.

I also knew that there were times when I wasn't a nice person to be around, and that I had given off a negative and self-centred vibe. I would no longer be putting time and energy into presenting an image to the world that wasn't true.

I would also no longer clothe myself in the emperor's new clothes, as close friends and family members must have known that all was not well.

Isn't it funny that sometimes you're the last to know and the last to be told? The elusive obvious escapes you, but others can see you for who and what you are and what you're like. It was a wonderful revelation.

Consternation

It was March, and over two months since I had woken up. I was eating healthily and was feeling great about myself. I even started to enjoy the dark, dreary cold winter mornings and had found acceptance in the feedback from the divine self with more ease.

It was as though I knew, and that part of me also knew, it was no longer about choice or preference; it was just the way it really is, was, had been and will be. Life isn't really asking for your permission; it never really needed it.

With my ego dissolved, during the awakening, I could see myself clearly for what I was. Life being life, and me being me, somewhere along the line I needed to consciously align myself with the flows of life itself by letting go more and being one with it.

I knew that life knew more than I did. I mean, I was one part of it, wasn't I? Life or God, as one. Or better yet, God knew what was happening, and the more we understand how it all works, the more we can align ourselves with the forces of life or with God—and one of the best ways of doing this is to be more out of your mind and into the present moment with God itself.

It wasn't all sunshine and rainbows. I also knew that somewhere along the line, I had done something terrible to myself on a personal level; something which I struggled with, as I knew that somewhere on the path before me, I had stopped believing in myself. I consider this to be one of my own greatest travesties. I even called it betrayal.

The irony was, I had done it to myself, and to me alone. I had allowed it to happen. It didn't happen on one single day or in one single event, but over time. Years. This is how I lost my edge, and with it my love of life. Love of the self.

As I sat there drinking my tea, it dawned on me that not only had I now acknowledged this as being true, but I had also accepted this as a truth. This also meant, from my personal perspective, that when I had stopped believing in my natural abilities to make life work for me and through me, I couldn't connect to the most powerful force consciously in the universe, my soul.

I had shut myself off; even though it kept supporting me, it was I who had through rage, anger, fear, loathing, self-neglect turned the other way. I'd been living in denial of what was truly going on in the world outside me, and that which is within all of us.

Therefore, my relationships had failed. I saw it for what it was, and I felt shame. I also knew that I had therefore come up short in some of the most fundamental areas of my life.

I realised that the wisdom contained within the download of the awakening experience was that this was what I needed to go through in order to understand what it was like to lose belief and confidence in myself, so that I could experience it.

I also knew that as a human being, as they say, we are in this world but not of it. As a human being, as a person, I was fully hooked, line and sinker.

The understanding of this was difficult to accept but at the same time, I knew that I had chosen this path and that it was necessary for me to experience it in its entirety. Meaning that for me to complete my journey to spiritual awakening, I had to experience myself fully as a spiritual being who is also having a human experience, because when it comes down to it, I am. I am both and also so much more, and so is everyone else.

I could sense the silence of the room around me, and the space within me expanded. Then, a wave of awareness moved through me. I instantaneously became fully aware of a newer level of awareness itself. I was moved by this experience. I felt 100% alive.

Then, by spiritual design, I was presented with a memory of my youth when I was cutting out a paper man. It was the exercise where you fold an A4 piece of paper over and over to the point that it's as small as it can be.

Then you cut out the outline of a paper man. Then you unfold it so that each one of the individual paper men are always connected to each other but at the same time, also singular.

What I was being shown symbolised not only the reincarnation of each day, but also each life that I had lived. In each life, I would experience different aspects of my being, and in this one where I had woken up, I had come to the end of this spiritual journey.

I needed to know what it felt like to lose hope, confidence, belief and love of myself. It was the last stage in this endless journey that I had been on for so long. I just didn't enjoy all of it. I mean, I know you're not meant to, but that's life, isn't it? It just is. Wow!

Meaning, I had tasted success. I had moments of momentous failure. I had fallen in and out of love on a regular basis. I had dreamt and had lived these wonderful dreams. I'd had nightmares, and lived them out in the real world. But through all of it, I continued to be myself, and at times, I hadn't been aware of it.

I had been used and I had used others to get my own way without a care in the world. I'd had highs and lows in my work life. I had made some great decisions, and there were times where I had lived out my delusions.

My life didn't have the type of onwards and upwards momentum that I had hoped for, or better yet, imagined it would be. At times, it was stop and start, then repeating itself, like a vicious cycle at times, not holistic virtuous perpetual motion.

It felt like one foot on the speed pedal and another on the brakes. It wasn't what I'd wanted it to be; a smooth, seamless journey of love, success, money and a fantastic lifestyle.

It was like watching a heartbeat monitor. I was either up or then I was down, and then there was a gradual climb up the mountain followed by a steep decline, and I found that my emotions seemed to be running in parallel with that. In fact, they were.

I felt like I was on the outside looking in, and not on the inside looking out.

With the continuation of the acknowledgement within myself, I hadn't noticed it at first, due to the subtleness of its own nature, that when we don't act on our truest and inner desire to live a life as simply being ourselves and not allowing any of our self-negative doubting thoughts to get in our way, we can rise above the normality and be our truest and beautiful and divine selves. To put it simply, just being yourself.

I hadn't acknowledged that being myself was the key. It always had been. It was so simple that I just couldn't see it or feel it.

Are you ready to continue, or would you like more time? If we are candid and honest with each other, my young friend, you have had a life that others would dream of. You have had experiences that others could only read about in magazines.

You chose this with your eyes wide open, and now you're realising that it came with all the attachments and the consequences that go with it.

I nodded my head. 'It's such a mess,' I said. 'I mean, my life was a car wreck, it's a fucking mess, how the fuck could I allow this to happen?'

I could feel the anger within me build up; the moment of pure awareness was gone, and I could feel the anger move literally through my entire being. It then changed to something that I could only label as hate; it spewed forth from within, like a raging torrent.

I didn't realise how much was contained within and was now being released from within me. I felt all my energy drain outside me. I was exhausted and felt horrible. It was quiet. I sat down and closed my eyes. I could now see clearly what I had done to myself.

'Where were you? How could you allow this to happen to me?' I wanted to distance myself immediately from it.

I love your mess, the voice told me. *I love what you've done with your life. I accept all of it. I love the fact you lived it in a way that suited you. I love the fact you went out there and lived as you, literally as you.*

I love the fact you went all the way and you backed yourself. I love the way you invested in your own life journey. I love the fact you went for it rather than talked about it.

You chose this path, this way, you intentionally chose it this way, this was of your own making, I get it. I really do. I love you.

I was moved to tears, and I broke down.

Can I tell you something else? It's not every day that one of you actually wakes up. It's rare, a full spiritual awakening is incredibly rare; there haven't been many of you who actually have, but you've hit the jackpot, you've won the ultimate prize.

It wasn't easy, I get it, I really do. I was with you all the time, every second, every minute, every step of the way, every word, every thought, every deed, I was with you all the time.

I loved you enough to allow you to have the experience that you desired, even when I knew it wasn't in your own best interest, but in the end it was. Even more so, why would I intervene, when this is what you have chosen for yourself?

True love has no limitations. You really went for it. The last three years have been difficult, but it was necessary, you had to go through this, this was a part of the journey to awakening, this was needed in order for you to truly understand, there was no other way for you as you, this is it, this is the real deal.

I don't play small with the universe. I never have, nor will I ever. Nor have you. This is it. I am everywhere, including inside you and outside you. Also, I know what you're like. What you're really like.

This experience works, it's worked for millions and millions of years on your planet, I really do know what I'm doing. I was there at the beginning because I am the beginning. I was the first word ever spoken. I was the first thought ever thought. I was the first action ever taken. I was the first breath.

It was I who brought the universe, and all contained within it, to being. I was the first song that was ever sung. I am the Alpha and the Omega. I am the Lion and the Lamb.

Have faith, little one. I know that you do, otherwise you wouldn't be awake, and we wouldn't be having this conversation, so pick yourself up and let's go, let's move forward. You're so close to the end of this, let's keep on going, you are made of sterner stuff.

So, I did, we continued to the end of the morning, and in the afternoon, I rested. My soul was at rest, and then I slept.

When I woke up, I asked the voice, 'I can't go back, can I?'

It replied, *there's nothing to go back to, you can only move forward.*

I nodded my head; and felt within a sense of loss. I could feel that I was being asked by the voice to accept that there was a deeper understanding to the words spoken.

'Okay?'

It's natural to ask, but no, since you know now what it's like to be awake. The thing is, it wouldn't serve you; you wouldn't go along with it either. You would reject it, rightfully, since the world as you know it wouldn't be as real as the world in which you are spiritually awake.

There is nothing left for you to experience, your journey home is complete. It will be you building bridges to others, since you know how difficult it is, and you know they wouldn't know, but you do, so as a master before you once said, "Be a light unto the world".

Be a light, my young friend, be you, let life do the rest. I love you, my young friend, love, love and be love and all will be revealed unto you. The universe will unfold before you, enlightened one. Walk it as you see fit.

It already has, and will continue to do so. Keep the faith, keep the truth within, live it as though it is. Because it is. It is the first mover. The prime mover, the first cause and the last.

Part Four:
Let There Be Light

I woke up the next morning, feeling the ebb and flow of energy coursing through my entire body. It was wonderful.

How do you feel this morning?

'I feel great.'

Can I tell you something? It's quite important.

'Yes, of course.'

Do you remember when I asked you about letting go, and you did?

I responded, 'Yes, I remember.'

Do you trust me?

I said, 'Yes.'

That's great, because I need you to know something. Today, I need you to let go because I don't want you to get hurt. Can you do that for me?

I said, 'Yes.' Then I moved to the front of the bed. I felt the stillness and silence within the room.

Please close your eyes, the voice said. Then the voice moved from the left and then to the right of me at unbelievable speed, and I felt myself go in both directions, to the left and then to the right.

I could feel my mind swaying as I felt it slowly becoming disintegrated. I tried to find relief as I felt this surge of energy course through me. I was holding on to my mind with all my might, but it wasn't working.

It was like watching a programme on TV, but as you watch the TV, it starts to slide at 45 degrees right in front of you and you don't know why and what the hell is happening. I started to panic, and then I felt anger and rage, but a feeling more like fear came through me.

I was ready to fight, I was ready to die. I surprised myself because I knew deep down inside that I couldn't win. Deep down within the recess of my own being, something primal was buried inside of me and it wanted to live.

The urge to survive screamed from within me. I never knew that it was there. Deep down within my soul, I wanted to live. I thought, *fuck it, bring it on.* My body tensed up and the fear become unbearable, but within the fear, the urge to live was stronger.

I really don't want to hurt you.

'Stop it then,' I shouted.

I love you, please let go.

So, I did. My mind dropped away and it ceased to exist. I felt peace and quiet. I felt no loss. I have never ever felt such peace before. I could feel life's energy coursing through my body.

It had always been there before, but now I could feel it. I could hear the wind outside and felt a more profound sense of connection with life. The world felt anew and alive at the same time. My face felt lighter, and I felt relaxed.

I felt a more profound sense of calmness wash over me. This sense and feeling of calmness was small at first, but then it gathered pace as it moved throughout my entire being; and in a single moment, I disappeared.

Literally, the old version of myself was gone, and a new version of myself was in the process of being created. The enlightened side presented the image of a moth being transformed into a butterfly. I could see and feel all those parts of me coming through, and something new and magnificent was being created.

I was wondering why I was keeping elements of my past life, and was informed by the divine voice, *you need it in order to survive in the world that you and the others have created.*

The change continued, and then I was shown a light that moved through me and then out of me. It was like watching how a pendulum works; the light seems to move through me from side to side, and I was at the centre of it.

I didn't understand what was being shown, and then the divine self spoke, *that's also what you are. You wanted to know what you're made of. You are so much more than just a physical being with a mind and a soul. Your science has only scratched the surface of knowing this to be true.*

I nodded. I asked, 'Can you show me that again, as I struggled with what I was seeing?' Again and again, I was shown the light that was blue and white move in and out of me.

I stared at where I had been down; it was as though I seemed to straddle all the different levels at once, but I only knew myself as a physical being with a mind.

I asked, 'Am I straddling different levels all at once, or do I exist in various levels/planes of existence all at the same time?'

What you are experiencing and witnessing is all those parts of yourself that make up who you are. You are a multi-dimensional being, and on one of the dimensions you have physical form. Your physical form, known as the human body, has a finite lifespan.

Like the unfolding of the paper man, you drop one body but then move seamlessly and effortlessly into the next. It is you who breathes life into each one of your individual forms.

I am using the words, stories and concepts from the source material that you've accumulated during your current life journey to best describe who you really are; and what I'm really doing is reminding you of this.

I was then shown the cover of a science book that I'd had when I was young; the cover of the book showed a ray of light hitting a prism-like triangle, and once the light went through it, the beam of light split into the different colours of the rainbow on the other side.

I realised that light was moving through me in a similar way, and what I was being shown was my own internal movable parts, including the divine self.

I was also a being of light. I looked substantially larger than I thought I was. I seemed to exist in more places than my eye could see and that my mind could comprehend. When I was one with myself, I and the light seemed to become whole. I am one and I am one with life itself, in all its shapes and in all its forms. We are one, you and I.

I was also a complete individual that consisted of many parts, and I had been experiencing each component at different times of my life. I no longer viewed myself as only a physical being or just a spiritual being.

The concept of a soul and a mind were just that, concepts, but without them, I wouldn't have been able to understand each of the unique parts of me. I was also a being who was spiritual by nature but with a physical human form and a mind to go with it.

I just hadn't realised that it was so externally focused. I hadn't the awareness to realise that it was I who was the thinker, the viewer and creator of my own experience; and that I was also using my mind as a tool with the external world.

With this new understanding, my perspective instantly changed, and it felt like life itself changed its understanding of me. I could feel the flow of infinite intelligence through me.

It is a reciprocal process. I seemed to exist in many places all at once, except I was still me being me; being myself all at the same time.

'How does that work?' I asked.

It just does. Over time, more will be revealed and you will be shown, and your understanding of how life works will grow in accordance with where you are on this new life journey that you are now embarking on.

No thoughts are required. You have been viewing yourself from the outside using your senses and the experiences that you have developed. You have used the knowledge and the insights that you have gained through your journey in life, and this in turn has made up the ever-moving canvas of your own internally-driven reality.

At that moment, I came to the realisation that I had only perceived myself as the image projected through my mind. How I talked and how I moved through life in my physical form, and the ideas that I held about myself, had been shaped through all the small moments as I experienced myself in real-time.

I just didn't know it. I also experienced myself on different levels beyond the physical form and beyond the mind.

My first impression was that I straddled multiple dimensions all at once, but I would later realise that all those dimensions which I had just witnessed or better yet reconnected to consciously were also a part of me.

Some of my beliefs and values weren't even mine to begin with. It was as though I had borrowed them until I was ready to release them, or in some cases, outgrew them as they no longer served me, and I would then create my own through my experiences, as I lived those of life.

It was as though the foundation of my character and personality had been shaped at a young age based on my parents' beliefs and values, and I had unconsciously adopted them, accepted them as my own without understanding the full implications of doing so.

I was more than the total sum of what I appeared to be. I was able to access within each experience the insight, the wisdom and the knowledge I needed to move forward.

I was able to shape and form the outlook of my own personal reality through each one of the experiences that I had created within myself with the full utilisation of my mind. Even if it wasn't real from the outside in, it was right for me from the inside out.

Each of the memories that I had created were of my own making. I was the creator of my own internal experiences, although I hadn't really registered this consciously. It had never ever occurred to me that I was doing this to myself all the time. I was stunned.

Since I wasn't experiencing any emotional attachments or residual value from these specific moments, I didn't feel any pain. Nor did I feel fear or joy or embarrassment; nor love. Just a sense of knowing my own inner truth about me. And it was done instantaneously.

I was elevated to a whole new level of life's understanding. I knew close to everything that had taken place in my own life, and at a fundamental level, the reasons why. Held within the why moments, I was able to piece and glue together how I had become the person that I was, and I knew the reasons for it.

The last part of the veil had been lifted fully. The visor was finally off. Before, in December, it had been put aside so that I could naturally and easily connect with the divine self and life itself.

Now all the questions that I had been searching for in my internal struggles had been answered. It was liberating. I had been set free. I really did have a conscious choice. I always did. But I now understood my idea of balance, the Ying and Yang of my life journey.

Then I heard a voice from within, *I am the Lion and the Lamb. I am the first and the last thought. I was there at the beginning, and I will be there at the end of time. I am beyond time. I am beyond forms as I am all forms. I was the first light.*

The first word ever spoken. I am the Alpha and the Omega. I am the wind that whispers in the desert and in the mountains. I am that which I am. I am the voice that spoke to the prophets in the desert, on the mountain tops, in the rain, and will always speak to those who want to hear and experience the truth.

I am life. I am one with all.

Renaissance

When I woke up the next day, I could still feel the sense of calm and inner peace within me. I sat down on the couch and closed my eyes and connected to the awareness of the outside world.

I felt perfectly at peace. I stayed there and enjoyed being myself. No sound, no noise, no thoughts, it felt beautiful.

When I opened my eyes, I could feel and see that the flat itself felt more spacious. I continued to look around the apartment and noticed that I had a hi-fi system gathering dust in the corner as it hadn't been used for years. So, I turned it on and listened to classical music. It was divine.

As I closed my eyes, the divine self brought into my awareness each of the musical instruments that were playing. One by one, they appeared before me, distinct, clear, and I could how hear the unique sound of each instrument. I laughed and opened my eyes.

Are you ready for more change? This time the divine voice was more precise than before, and I said, 'Yes.'

As you have been through the change internally, will you choose to make the change externally? Any item of your possessions from your previous way of living and associated with your previous way of being is to be removed, as it's a remnant of your past and is no longer you. All must go.

If you decide to continue with your current work, you will need an attire that is associated with your new level in your work life, and not the level you once thought. The idea of what you thought you were and the images and memories that you previously created for yourself will no longer work or serve you.

This year is going to be an enjoyable and exciting year for you, and you will be surprised how much you have changed.

You will also continue to expand your level of awareness and consciousness of being awake, and this will present its own healthy and vibrant challenges.

So, remember to relax into the experience and just be you. You will notice that being you works perfectly well all the time.

Concepts will no longer hold their sway over you; you will only be interested in what you are experiencing, what you would consider to be "real". Real life will hold you in its thrall.

When you're dealing with other human beings, you will be continuously reminded of who and what you are in that moment, real-time, not the fabrication of the mind time; and you will notice the implications of your own choices.

So be you, and allow others to be themselves. It worked perfectly well for you, and you came home spiritually.

We are one, you and I! Till the end of time and beyond If you allow the path beneath you to unfold naturally, then the experience that you are having will be natural and relative to you, and to you alone. As it is for you, so it is for others.

So, let us begin. You have found in your awakening your own middle path, which you understood to be the movement of the centre of yourself that exists between the options of choice that you created.

You are now aware of the effects of your own inner creativity and the decisions that you have made. You weren't, at times, overly impressed by the actions that you took, nor some of the choices that you made, nor on some occasions, the lack of decisions taken.

But you accepted that those choices that you created, and the decisions made, were yours alone to make. You have accepted the truth of what you have created, and in doing so, this in turn set into motion the insight that is contained within each given moment.

This insight assisted you in making better conscious decisions, that elevated you to a whole new level of awareness and in turn understanding of who and what you are in the process of living life itself.

You then opened yourself up to new ideas and beliefs, since you were able to release yourself from your old ideas and thought patterns. You also forgave yourself, even when you didn't need to.

So, this ends the process of your awakening and your spiritual enlightenment. My job is now done. Allow yourself the time to heal and be you. Remember, my young friend, I have been with you always; from your first breath and step into this world.

I have been there when you have been magnificent, and when you have been down in life. If you need to find me, you will find me everywhere. You just need to look and keep an open mind about things.

I am excited for the two of us about what you are about to embark on and what you intend to do with your knowledge, wisdom and insight.

You will always find me in the silence; and when you are there, I will find you. Love and peace, little one, love and peace.